Why Skies are Blue and Parrots Talk

Answers to the Questions You've Always Wanted to Ask

Andrew Thompson

JOHN BLAKE

Published by John Blake Publishing Ltd,
3, Bramber Court, 2 Bramber Road,
London W14 9PB, England

www.blake.co.uk

First published in Hardback in 2005

ISBN 1 84454 187 8

British Library Cataloguing-in-Publication Data:

A catalogue record for this book is available from the British Library.

Design by www.envydesign.co.uk

Printed in Great Britain by Creative Print and Design, Wales

1 3 5 7 9 10 8 6 4 2

Papers used by John Blake Publishing are natural, recyclable products
made from wood grown in sustainable forests. The manufacturing processes
conform to the environmental regulations of the country of origin.

Every attempt has been made to contact the relevant copyright-holders,
but some were unobtainable. We would be grateful if the appropriate
people could contact us.

To Mum, for teaching me to seek out answers.
And to Dad, for asking the questions to begin with.

CONTENTS

WHY IS THE SKY BLUE?

One of the most commonly seen sights is the blue sky, yet what's not widely known is what makes it blue.

The sun emits light that travels through space towards Earth. Because space is a vacuum (ie it has no atmosphere), the light remains largely undisturbed until it nears the Earth, whose atmosphere is made up of a mixture of gas molecules (mainly oxygen and nitrogen) and other materials. The closer you get to the Earth, the thicker the atmosphere.

Light from the sun appears white but is in fact a combination of colours, and the range of these colours that are visible to the human eye – from red to violet, by way of orange, yellow, green, blue and indigo – is shown when light is passed through a prism. These different colours have different wavelengths and energies, with violet having the shortest wavelength and highest energy and red having the longest wavelength and lowest energy.

As light hits the Earth's atmosphere, the different colours react in different ways. Some of them get absorbed by the gas molecules while others do not. Most of the longer-wavelength colours (such as red and orange) pass straight through the atmosphere and are unaffected, while many of the shorter-wavelength colours (such as violet and blue) get absorbed by the gas molecules, because the wavelengths (ie the distance between the peaks of each wave) of these colours are similar in size to the diameter of an atom of oxygen. The gas molecules then radiate these colours and scatter them across the sky, causing the sky to appear blue.

The reason why we perceive the sky as blue and not violet is because our eyes are more sensitive to blue.

WHY ARE MOTHS ATTRACTED TO LIGHTS?
It's commonly known that moths are attracted to bright lightbulbs and torches and often circle them, giving rise to the saying 'like moths to a flame'. There are a number of theories as to why moths engage in this often life-threatening practice.

The traditional hypothesis is that moths mistake the light source for the moon. Moths are thought to migrate long distances, and it is believed that they use the moon to navigate on their journeys, it being a relatively stationary reference point from which to gauge direction. They can travel in straight lines by maintaining a constant angle to the moon. When the moth mistakes an artificial light source for the moon, it continues to keep a constant angle to the light. However, because of its close proximity to the light, this results in it spiralling towards it in a confused state.

While it's accepted that moths do indeed use the moon to navigate, the problem with the idea that moths mistake lights for the moon is that they tend to fly directly to a light and then spiral around it, rather than spiralling towards it as soon as they spot it.

A second theory is that moths fly towards lights in an attempt to keep warm. However, this is discredited because it turns out that moths are more attracted to ultra-violet lightbulbs than those emitting normal visible light, which are warmer. In fact, moths are more sensitive to certain wavelengths of light – for example, they are more attracted to the colours in white light than to yellow.

A third theory – and the most compelling – is that moths are initially attracted to a light source and will fly directly towards it, but then, once there, will try to avoid the light and seek darkness (perhaps because they're nocturnal creatures). As a result of a peculiarity in the moths' vision, they perceive that the darkest place in the sky is an area about 1ft from the light source. As a safety mechanism, the moth seeks out this darkest place and remains there, causing it to circle the light frantically within the dark band.

CAN THE GREAT WALL OF CHINA BE SEEN FROM SPACE?

It's commonly said that the Great Wall of China is the only manmade structure that can be seen with the naked eye from space or the moon. This proposition has been perpetuated in many sources: it's a question in the board game Trivial Pursuit, it has been contained in schoolbooks across the world and it was stated as being the case by Ed Harris in the 1998 movie *The Truman Show*. In addition, Richard Halliburton's *Second Book Of Marvels* makes such a claim, despite the fact that this book was first published in 1938, before man launched any satellites!

One school of thought is that the claim was made to convey the enormous scale of the Wall and the vastness of man's achievement in building it. It is now accepted that the proposition is false.

Many large-scale manmade objects, such as highways, airports, buildings and ships, *can* be seen with the naked eye, as can the Great Wall itself, but only from low Earth orbit (up to about 200 miles above sea level). The Wall's width ranges from about five to ten metres but, when dust storms hit it, it becomes more visible at this close range. However, no manmade structures at all are visible with the naked eye above an altitude of a few thousand miles, and certainly not from the moon, which is about 240,000 miles away and from which entire continents and oceans are barely visible without mechanical assistance. These facts have been confirmed by a number of astronauts who have left the question beyond any doubt.

WHY WERE NECK TIES INVENTED?

It is often questioned why such a seemingly useless item of apparel as the neck tie was ever invented. It's thought by some anthropologists that it might well have been the first item of clothing ever worn, taking the form of a strip of fur around the necks of our ancestors. However, the earliest evidence of the wearing of neck ties was by the Chinese. China's first emperor, Shih Huang Ti, was afraid of death and commanded that replicas of his army personnel be laid to rest with him for protection. He died in 210 BC, and when his tomb was rediscovered in 1974 the intricately detailed terracotta replicas preserved therein each wore neck cloths or ties.

Neck ties were also present in Roman times. In AD 113, after one of his victories, the emperor Trajan erected a marble column bearing reliefs that feature thousands of soldiers, many of whom are wearing neck ties. It's thought by some that these soldiers wore neck ties to guard against cold weather or to absorb sweat.

While neck ties have been around in one form or another for millennia, it was because of the Croatians in the seventeenth century that wearing them became a statement of fashion. After helping in a victory against the Hapsburg Empire, thousands of soldiers were presented to King Louis XIV in Paris, among them a regiment of Croatian marines, some of whom wore colourful cravats. These embellishments appealed to the French, who had never seen such an article of clothing and who were soon wearing similar cravats. Until the French Revolution in 1789, the French maintained an elite regiment known as the Cravate Royale, and the word 'cravat' itself is from the French word 'cravate', meaning 'Croatian'.

It wasn't long before the wearing of neck ties spread. In 1660, Charles II returned to England from exile and reclaimed the throne that he lost during the Civil War. He was followed by aristocrats who brought the cravat to England, whereupon it developed into the neck tie, became popular and spread throughout Europe, then America and then the rest of the world.

WHAT CAUSES JET LAG AND HOW CAN IT BE PREVENTED AND CURED?

Jet lag, or desynchronosis, is a condition that's caused by crossing time zones during air travel. It is said to be a symptom of the disruption of the body's circadian rhythms – ie the day/night light/dark cycle, which controls the timing of bodily functions such as when you sleep and eat.

Other contributing factors to jet lag are the dry atmosphere of planes and the lack of fresh air; the discomfort caused by cramped conditions; swelling caused by cabin pressure; the food and drink consumed in transit; and the direction of travel. North/south travel doesn't result in jet lag, because the time zone remains the same, while some suggest that flying east results in the worst jet lag, as it accelerates the passage through the time zones and that, because time is 'lost', there is less time to 'absorb' (the human body is more adept at compensating for enduring longer days than shorter ones). Others maintain that jet lag is greater when travelling away from your normal time zone than towards it.

The symptoms of jet lag are irregular sleep

patterns and insomnia, fatigue, confusion and disorientation, irritability, headaches, nausea, dehydration and a loss of appetite. It's estimated that one day of recovery time is needed for every one-hour time zone crossed.

The effects of jet lag can be reduced in various ways. For example, before a flight you should be well rested and relaxed. Plenty of exercise before a flight can help, too, and no alcohol should be consumed beforehand, though some medical professionals suggest the taking of certain drugs and hormonal supplements.

To reduce the effects of jet lag while in the air, drink plenty of water and avoid alcohol (it's thought that the effects of alcohol are more pronounced at high altitudes) and caffeine-based drinks. Get as much exercise as possible by stretching in your seat or walking about the plane. Remove your shoes and get comfortable. Adjusting your watch to the new time zone can also be psychologically beneficial.

Once you're on the ground, have a shower to get your blood moving, drink plenty of water and try to adapt to the environment of the new time zone as quickly as possible. Maximising your exposure to the sun can help you to adjust to your new environment, so you shouldn't sleep upon arrival; instead, wait until night.

WHY DO WE YAWN AND WHY IS IT CONTAGIOUS?

It has traditionally been thought that yawning is an involuntary reflex whose aim is to draw more oxygen into our bloodstreams and remove a build-up of carbon dioxide. This theory was fuelled by the notion that when people are bored or tired their breathing slows, resulting in a lack of oxygen, which causes them to yawn. However, research based on exercise suggests that this theory is incorrect. In tests, it was discovered that people's yawning rates were not altered during exercise, despite an increase in the breathing rate and levels of oxygen in the bloodstream. In addition, athletes often yawn before big events, which is unlikely to be as a result of boredom or a reduced level of breathing. It has also been found that foetuses yawn in the womb, even though they don't breathe oxygen into their lungs until after birth.

It has been suggested that people yawn to stretch the lungs, jaw and facial muscles, which increases the heart rate and makes a person feel more awake, although this suggestion is largely posited on the fact that a stifled yawn that does not stretch the jaw is unsatisfying. Other theories are that yawning is used to regulate body temperature or is caused by a variation in certain chemicals, such as dopamine, in the brain. It is now accepted that the exact reasons why we yawn are unknown.

It's also not known why yawning is contagious. One theory is that we have evolved to yawn when others around us do because our early ancestors used yawning to co-ordinate social behaviour or to build rapport in a group. When one person yawned to signal something, such as it being time to sleep, the rest of the group also yawned in agreement and the members' activities were synchronised.

Yawning might also have been used to bare the teeth to intimidate enemies, so that, when one member of the group yawned, the rest followed suit. This has carried through to modern times, when the suggestive power of yawning is still contagious. Lending weight to this theory is the fact that babies, who are unaware of social codes, don't yawn contagiously until they're about one year old.

WHAT IS A BLUE MOON?

'Once in a blue moon' is an expression for something that rarely happens, and of course it begs the question, what is a blue moon?

A literal blue moon occurs when enough smoke or dust is present in the atmosphere to make the moon appear blue. This occurred back in 1883, when the Indonesian volcano Krakatoa exploded, and in 1950, when masses of smoke from Canadian bush fires filled the air.

The first use of the expression was in a 1528 book, where a blue moon referred to something that would never happen, similar to the saying 'if the moon was made of green cheese'. In the 1700s, meanwhile, saying 'I'll marry you when the moon is blue' was not a marriage proposal but a statement denying that there was any chance of marriage.

The expression 'once in a blue moon' came to mean something that happened only occasionally. An edition of *The Maine Farmers' Almanac* from the 1800s defined a blue moon as the third of four full moons that occurred in a season. The first full moon was known as Lenten Moon, the second was known as Paschal Moon and the third – if it did appear, which was a rarity – was known as Blue Moon, and it's from the *Almanac* that the modern meaning of the expression is derived.

In March 1946, the author of a *Sky & Telescope* magazine article misinterpreted the reference to the Blue Moon in the 1937 edition of the *Almanac*, interpreting the Blue Moon to be the second full moon in a single calendar month, and this interpretation of the term became popular and still exists today. In fact, the average interval between full moons – ie the lunar month – is twenty-nine and a half days, which is shorter than the average calendar month of thirty and a half days. This makes two full moons in the one month possible but rare. A blue moon generally happens forty-one times every century, which equates to once every two and a half years. It can occur in any month except February (which is too short) and is most likely to happen in either January or March, because they each contain thirty-one days and are separated by February. The last blue moon was in November 2001.

WHAT ARE THE ORIGINS OF BOXING DAY?

Boxing Day – also known as St Stephen's Day, after the first Christian martyr, who was one of Jesus's disciples – is celebrated on 26 December, and there are a number of ill-founded theories as to why it's celebrated. One is that it started because of the need to remove empty Christmas Day present boxes from the house, while another is that it was the day during which unwanted Christmas gifts were returned to their boxes. A further incorrect theory is that its name derived from the box kept on board a ship in which to collect donations to the parish priest, to be given out on the day after Christmas.

In fact, Boxing Day originated in England under Queen Victoria in the mid-nineteenth century. It began as a holiday on the day after Christmas during which the upper classes gave tradespeople and servants money and goods in boxes, which gave the day its name. While presents exchanged between members of the upper classes were given on Christmas Day, the servants were employed to ensure the smooth running of this day and so had to wait until the following day to rest and receive their presents. This practice of giving gifts in boxes on 26 December continued until the mid-twentieth century for people who provided services, such as postmen and rubbish collectors.

Combined with this delayed exchanging of gifts, 26 December was the date on which churches would traditionally open their alms boxes (receptacles containing monetary donations from the more affluent people) to the poor.

Today, Boxing Day is a holiday in the UK and many of the Commonwealth nations, but people no longer exchange gifts on the day and, of course, alms boxes no longer exist.

DO YOU GET WET WHEN WALKING IN THE RAIN THAN YOU DO WHEN RUNNING?

The question of whether people will get wetter if they walk through the rain than if they run through it has been the subject of much bar-room discussion. More than that, scientists have been considering the problem for many years, and have concluded that many factors can contribute to which method of progress exposes a person to more rain. Some factors are the speed and intensity of the rain, the build of the person, the direction and angle of the rain and the distance travelled.

The main reason for the debate is the fact that raindrops generally hit both the head and the front of the body. It has been thought that, because a runner will be in the rain for a shorter period than a walker will, fewer drops will hit his or her head, and this is a generally agreed-upon hypothesis. However, some believe that a runner will be hit with more drops on the front of the body because of his or her increased velocity when running. The balance of these two factors has been put to the test scientifically.

A number of experiments have been performed to determine the best way of keeping dry when moving in the rain, most of which have resulted in a running person ending up less wet than a walking person. While some experiments found that the number of drops per second that a runner received was the same as for a walker (because the runner was hit more on the front but less on the head), the runner was in the rain for a shorter period and so got hit with fewer drops overall. A number of experiments counting the actual number of drops that hit both a runner and a walker found that the runner received far fewer head drops, but that the front drops for the runner and walker were the same, which again resulted in the runner getting less wet.

In one experiment, the runner ended up getting 40 per cent less wet, while in another this figure was reduced to 10 per cent. A 1997 experiment found that running in a light rain with no wind resulted in the runner getting 16 per cent less wet, while leaning forward and running fast in heavy rain being driven by wind resulted in the runner getting 44 per cent less wet. On the basis of these experiments, it's possible to determine that running is always the best option, particularly in heavy rain.

DOES WATER TRAVEL DOWN THE PLUGHOLE IN DIFFERENT DIRECTIONS IN THE NORTHERN AND SOUTHERN HEMISPHERES?

Folklore states that water drains down the sink in an anti-clockwise direction in the northern hemisphere and a clockwise direction in the southern hemisphere, supposedly owing to a physical phenomenon called the Coriolis effect. Named after a French engineer, this effect is caused by the Earth's rotation subjecting a twisting force to fluids flowing along its surface. The force occurs over large distances and periods of time, and is reversed in the two hemispheres, which explains why macroevents such as hurricanes rotate in opposite directions depending on where they are. When it comes to small bodies of water, such as those contained by a sink or bath, these are far too insignificant to be effected in any noticeable way by Coriolis forces.

The direction in which water drains down sinks and bathtubs depends on the shape and surface of the bowl and drain (most aren't completely flat), the configuration of the taps and the way in which the water is poured in. Depending on these factors alone, water can drain down in either direction in either hemisphere. If water is swirled into the drain in a clockwise direction, it's likely to carry on draining in that direction.

The reason for the enduring myth is most likely because it has repeatedly been quoted on television programmes and in textbooks.

IS ONE DOG YEAR EQUAL TO SEVEN HUMAN YEARS?

The age-old adage that one dog year equals seven human years derives from the simple mathematical division of the average human lifespan by the average canine lifespan.

It's true that dogs do age much faster than humans

because of their higher metabolic rate; generally speaking, the larger the mammal, the slower the metabolism and the longer the life. However, it's now generally accepted that the seven-to-one rule of thumb for a dog's 'realistic' age is inaccurate; for instance, it's not uncommon for dogs to live to the age of fifteen, but very few humans live to 105.

It's believed that the seven-year rule should not be applied proportionally, and that, while it might be appropriate for the middle section of a dog's life, the beginning or final developmental phases cannot be correlated to those of a human. A dog tends to be fully sized and sexually mature at the age of one, but the same cannot be said of a human of seven. A more accurate method of calculating a dog's 'realistic' age is to allocate twenty-one years for the first year (ie when dog and human both reach adulthood) and then four years for every additional year.

The size and breed of a dog are also factors that impact on how fast it ages. Larger dogs age the fastest, so even the above rule cannot be applied to all breeds of dogs. In fact, the older the dog, the more accurate the seven-to-one ratio becomes. Roughly, a large ten-year-old dog is considered to be seventy-eight, whereas a small ten-year-old dog would be fifty-six.

HOW DID LORD'S, THE FAMOUS HOME OF CRICKET, GET ITS NAME?

It's not uncommon for people to assume that the famous London cricket ground of Lord's – known by lovers of the game as the home of cricket – was named after the aristocracy at the time, considering how closely the game was associated with the upper classes. In fact, Lord's was named after a man named Thomas Lord, who in the eighteenth century was approached to build the ground by English noblemen cricketers who didn't like playing in front of the growing crowds that were drawn by the game's increasing popularity. Lord was a Yorkshireman, and he travelled down to London in 1787 to set up a private cricket club for these nobles who tired of displaying their prowess before members of lower castes.

The first match played at Lord's was between Essex and Middlesex in 1787, a year before the rules of cricket were formally drawn up. The ground was originally at Marylebone, and thus the MCC (Marylebone Cricket Club) was established, which owns Lord's to this day. The ground was moved twice, however, and in 1814 Lord took the original turf to St John's Wood, where the ground remains, on the site of a former duck pond.

The first groundsman was appointed at Lord's in 1864 and, after fire destroyed the original pavilion, a new one was built in 1889. This pavilion now houses the MCC Library and the Museum, which holds various memorabilia, including the urn containing the Ashes.

WHY DO BUSES OFTEN COME IN THREES?

A common complaint of people who use public transport is that of waiting at a bus stop for ages and then three buses arrive all at once.

In fact, mathematicians have attempted to explain this everyday conundrum by means of applying complex formulae based on queuing models, correlation and renewal theories, random matrixes and bunching. However, the phenomenon can be explained in fairly simply terms.

Buses leave the depot at regular intervals, but the number of people waiting at the various bus stops tends to vary considerably, and it's these variations at the bus stops that play an important role in 'bus bunching'. For example, if there's an excessive number of passengers waiting at one bus stop, the first bus will take longer than normal to load these passengers. In this time, the second bus catches up a little. When this second bus arrives at the same stop, it's likely that there won't be as many passengers waiting, as most of them are on the first bus, so the second bus won't stay at the bus stop for as long. Also, because the first bus has taken longer at the first stop, it's likely that more passengers will be waiting at the next stop. The process then repeats itself, with the second bus eventually catching the first until they travel in tandem, acting as one. The longer the route, the more buses that are likely to join the convoy, although experiments have shown that the most common bunching number is two buses.

Despite there being such a scientific basis for bus bunching, some claim that it rarely occurs and that people forget how often single buses arrive.

WHY DO WOMEN TALK MORE THAN MEN DO, BUT CAN'T READ MAPS AS WELL AS MEN?

While all human brains consist of the same material – about 40 per cent grey matter and 60 per cent white matter – the brain of a man is significantly different from that of a woman. From studies conducted using intelligence tests, it has been determined that men use nearly seven times more grey matter than women do, whereas women use nine times more white matter than men do. The main functions of grey matter seem to lie in the disciplines of spatial awareness, including map-reading, mathematics and problem-solving, whereas white matter connects the processing centres of the brain and is important in the use of language, emotional thinking and the ability to do more than one thing at once.

Because women use more white brain matter, they tend to be better communicators. In fact, the female brain has a greater number of areas associated with communication than the male brain, which explains why women tend to use language as an emotional rapport-building device whereas men use language to exchange information and solve problems. On average, a woman says 7,000 words per day while a man says only 2,000.

The two hemispheres of the female brain are also linked more effectively than those of the male brain, and they're more closely connected, which explains how women are better able to multitask than men, who generally have to concentrate on one job at a time. This greater connectivity in the female brain is also thought to be the reason for so-called 'women's intuition'.

These differences are thought to have been brought about by the social roles adopted by men and women in our ancestors' time. Men, for instance, would go out hunting, often tracking their quarry for many days, which required problem-solving and navigation, whereas women needed to be more emotionally and linguistically attuned to protect their home and offspring. In fact, studies show that women with higher than average levels of the male hormone testosterone tend to be able to read maps more effectively than other women.

WHY DO PEOPLE NEED SLEEP?

The origins and purposes of sleep are still not fully understood, and experts have been arguing about them for millennia. Hippocrates, for instance, believed that sleep allowed blood to retreat within the body, while Aristotle thought that sleep was needed for digestion.

The amount of sleep that each person needs depends on his or her age and, without it, he or she can become irritable and unable to complete normal tasks, while prolonged periods without sleep can result in hallucinations and even death. Sleep, it seems, is necessary for our survival.

There are many theories that attempt to explain the function of sleep. Some believe that sleep shuts down and repairs neurones in the brain, allowing for the increased production of hormones and proteins necessary to rejuvenate the emotional and social functioning areas of our mind. Sleep is also thought to be vital for repairing the muscles and tissues of the body, as well as the nervous and immune systems, and a function for conserving energy. It's also believed that sleep provides the necessary physical environment for the brain to process information and organise our thoughts, and indeed things learned just prior to sleep are often more easily remembered. However, drugs such as alcohol alter certain stages of sleep, reducing its rejuvenative benefits.

It is thought that our present need for sleep stems directly from the behaviour of our ancestors, who would bed down in caves at night in order to avoid predators and because there was little else to do during the hours of darkness. As a result, we have evolved to depend on sleep.

IS THE DRINK RED BULL DANGEROUS?

Red Bull is the brand name of a canned soft drink that is marketed as an energy source and stimulant containing sugar, vitamin B, glucuronolactone, caffeine (around the same amount as in a cup of coffee) and a compound called taurine, which gives the drink its name.

In the early part of 2000, a number of people started questioning whether the drink was dangerous to human health, as there was a suggestion that one of its ingredients, glucuronolactone, was an artificial stimulant given to US troops in Vietnam in the 1960s to boost morale. It was said that the drug produced brain tumours and death in some of the soldiers, although there is no scientific evidence supporting this suggestion. However, in 2001, the drink was investigated by the Swedish National Food Administration after being connected to the deaths of three people.

Some experts are concerned about the inclusion of glucuronolactone and taurine in the drink. Glucuronolactone is a natural carbohydrate produced by the human metabolic system, but the amounts contained in each can of Red Bull are high enough to worry some people. A recent study found that more testing was needed to assess the dangers of glucuronolactone and taurine, but many think that high quantities could be dangerous to people. Experts are also concerned about the levels of caffeine in the drink, especially when it's mixed with alcohol, as it often is.

The sale of Red Bull as a normal soft drink is now prohibited in Denmark, France and Norway.

DO WE REALLY USE ONLY 10 PER CENT OF OUR BRAINS?

Psychologists in the early twentieth century commented that humans use only 10 per cent of their brains, and Albert Einstein also indicated that humans use only a small portion of the brain. It's a theory that has been propounded in television documentaries, magazines, advertisements and books over the past century. Psychics have also latched on to it as a possible explanation for paranormal behaviour, attributing unusual incidents to the workings of the unused portion of the brain. They profess that 90 per cent of our brains consists of untapped potential that is capable of remarkable feats.

Nearly all scientists now agree that the theory that we use only 10 per cent of our total brain function is completely unfounded. In fact, they question how this figure was arrived at in the first place and what areas of the brain are supposed to be redundant. The theory supposes that, if 90 per cent of the brain were removed, a person would still be able to function normally, whereas in reality it is known that damage to even a small area of the brain can result in physical devastation.

In addition, most significant disorders of the brain involve only a small and very specific area of the brain. If the 10 per cent argument was true, it's unlikely that so many problems would persistently occur in that area. And if we use only 10 per cent of our nerves and neurones in the brain, how would this be measured? Indeed, imaging of the brain in scans shows that all parts of the brain are used for different activities and that many areas of the brain are used for some complex activities or thought processes. Throughout the course of one day, most areas of the brain are active at some time, even during sleep. The 10 per cent theory suggests that a discrete area of the brain is not used, whereas scans reveal activity throughout the entire brain and not in any isolated segment. The final nail in the 10 per cent theory is the fact that neurosurgeons carefully map the brain before removing tumours so that they don't compromise other essential areas.

From an evolutionary perspective, it's highly unlikely that our comparatively larger brains would have evolved from our ancestors if the extra areas were surplus to requirements. In fact, there is absolutely no evidence to support the 10 per cent theory.

WHY DO PEOPLE OFTEN WAKE UP JUST BEFORE THE ALARM?

Some people find that, no matter what time they go to bed, they wake at the same time every morning, quite often just before their alarm clock sounds.

Scientists believe that a person wakes at the same time each day because of the body's circadian rhythms, the internal 'body clock' that regulates the cyclic processes of the body over a twenty-four-hour period. These rhythms are important in determining the sleep patterns of people and are thought to be predominantly internal (that is, not affected by external stimuli), being affected and largely defined by regular activity in people, which goes some way to explaining why people generally wake up at around the same time every day. Studies have also shown that a person's body temperature rises at the same time each morning, which is also linked to waking.

Waking just before the alarm is thought to be the work of the subconscious. People anticipate the time they're going to wake up, and this anticipation makes them wake just before the alarm goes off. Both waking and the sound of the alarm cause stress, so the subconscious sets a time of waking just before the alarm goes off. The theory is that, if people think of an exact time they are going to awaken and imagine themselves waking at that time, the subconscious takes over while they're asleep and makes this happen. Indeed, some studies have shown an increase in certain hormones in the body that wake a person in circumstances when they were aware of the time that the alarm was due to go off, caused by the subconscious anticipating this time and prompting the body to wake itself.

HOW DO MOBILE PHONES WORK?

A mobile phone is essentially a two-way radio, like a CB set, transmitting and receiving wireless radio-frequency signals. However, while a CB set is what's known as a 'simplex' device (ie two people can communicate at the same time but only one person can talk at once), a mobile phone is described as a 'duplex' device (ie it uses one frequency for transmitting and another for receiving, enabling people on either end of the line to talk and listen simultaneously). The radio signal from the phone is transmitted through the air to the antenna of the nearest base station, which contains equipment designed to emit radio transmissions and passes the signal to the network and then to its destination. Each base station covers an area of about ten square miles, known as a 'cell', which is why mobile phones are sometimes called cell or cellular phones.

Mobile-phone signals can reach only limited distances, which is why an intricate network of cells is needed to connect people at greater distances and why mobile phones don't work in remote areas that have no base stations. Each base station has a finite capacity to receive and transmit signals, and highly populated areas usually have a higher number of base stations to cope with the large number of users.

The reason why a mobile phone can be used while driving for many miles is because the signal moves from one base station to the next so that a number of base stations, and their cells, are utilised.

Mobile phones contain low-power transmitters and low-mass lithium-ion batteries that store a lot of power, two factors that enable them to be very small and light.

WAS THE 1969 MOON LANDING A FAKE?

On 21 July 1969, US astronauts Neil Armstrong and Buzz Aldrin became the first humans to set foot on the moon. Even today, however, some people believe that the moon landing was an elaborate hoax that was actually staged in a secret area of the Nevada desert.

There are conspiracy theories that supposedly support this claim, one such being that no footprints should have been left on the surface of the moon, as there's no moisture there to allow the dust to clump together to form prints. (The astronauts claimed that the ground was of a consistency similar to that of talcum powder, in which it is possible to leave footprints.) Others claim that, in the photographs taken on the supposedly lunar surface, objects cast a number of shadows, implying that they were taken with nearby multiple light sources when the only light source available to the astronauts was the sun. The theorists also question how all the photographs were of such high quality when they were taken by men in heavy suits with gloves. And how did they change the films? Who took the photo of Armstrong taking his first step on the moon? How come the flag he planted is shown as being well lit even on the side of it that's away from the light? And why are there no stars visible in any of the photos, or any trace of blasting from the rocket that carried the men down to the lunar surface? The fact that the American flag that is put in the ground flutters is also one of the theorist's compelling arguments, given that there is no atmosphere or wind on the moon, but the people who refute this say that the flag was moving because it had to be twisted into the ground. But what of the astronauts' golf shots that sliced, a phenomenon caused by airflow across the ball?

NASA has refused to comment significantly on any of these allegations, allowing the many photographs and lengths of video footage to speak for themselves, along with the testimonies of the many people involved in the project, none of whom has ever intimated that the landings were faked. More importantly, numerous samples were brought back from the Apollo 11 mission that have been tested by many independent institutions and found to be of extraterrestrial origin, some of them containing isotopes caused by nuclear reactions not normally found on Earth. The real truth, however, may never be known.

WHEN DID THE GAME ROCK, PAPER, SCISSORS BEGIN?

Rock, Paper, Scissors is a game of chance generally used to decide trivial matters between two people. Each participant shakes a fist three times, producing on the third shake either a clenched fist (Rock), an open hand (Paper) or two extended fingers (Scissors). Rock beats Scissors (because it can crush them), Paper beats Rock (because it can cover it) and Scissors beats Paper (because it can cut it). If the two players produce the same item, the game is replayed until the stalemate is broken.

Rock, Paper, Scissors is played in many countries and is known under many different names: in Japan, for instance, it is called Jan-Ken-Pon, while elsewhere it's often known as Roshambo, except in Italy, where it has been played since the early eighteenth century and is now known as Mora. Some countries have variants of the Rock, Paper and Scissors elements; in Indonesia, for example, they are an elephant, a person and an ant.

With such widespread popularity, there are many theories as to when and where this game began. Some believe that it has been played in Japan since 200 BC and migrated to Europe in the eighteenth century, while others believe it began with Celtic settlers in Portugal in 600 BC, after which it spread to Europe when the Romans invaded Spain in around AD 100.

While it's likely that the exact origin of the game will never be known owing to a lack of tangible evidence, the predominant theory is that it began on the Mediterranean coast and in the Orient thousands of years ago. Lending weight to this theory are Egyptian hieroglyphic paintings from 2000 BC that indicate a similar finger-and-fist guessing game.

WHY DO PEOPLE TWITCH AS THEY FALL ASLEEP?

It's a widely known fact that some people twitch and jump suddenly as they are falling asleep, and these twitches are known as *hypnagogic myoclonis*, where 'hypnagogic' refers to sleep and 'myoclonis' refers to any type of involuntary muscle spasm. Twitching generally occurs during the early stages of very light sleep as a person is drifting off to sleep, and for this reason such spasms are also called 'sleep starts'.

While it's not known exactly what causes the twitches, they are the result of sudden muscle contractions that some scientists believe are related to anxiety or caused by a faint stimulus, such as a noise or a touch. Vivid dreaming in the early stages of sleep may also cause twitching (dreaming about falling, for example, often results in twitching), while muscle fatigue can be another contributory factor.

Other scientists believe that some forms of

twitching are caused by a disruption of two particular neurotransmitters in the brain: serotonin, which constricts blood vessels and induces sleep, and gamma-aminobutyic acid, which helps to control the muscles. It's thought that these neurotransmitters get disrupted while the sleepy brain ceases to control the body's motor functions, resulting in twitching.

While myoclonic jerks can be a symptom of a disease such as multiple sclerosis or Parkinson's and Alzheimer's syndrome, they are generally harmless and common in many people. On most occasions, the person experiencing the twitching is unaware that it's happening and doesn't remember it afterwards.

WHAT IS THE COMMON COLD AND HOW IS IT CURED?

The common cold is a mild viral disease that infects the nose, throat and respiratory system, generally bringing about congestion of the nose, sneezing, coughing and breathing difficulties, which are symptoms caused by the body's attempts to expel the virus. The cold differs from influenza (ie the flu), which is a more severe viral infection that also results in fevers, chills and muscular aches.

The common cold is the most common disease in humans and is caused by many viruses that infect the body, entering the cells in the nose, where they multiply. The most common of these viruses are the rhinoviruses. Vaccination against them is impractical because of the large number of different viruses that can cause a cold, combined with the fact that they can also mutate to form new viruses.

A cold is contagious during the first two to four days after symptoms first appear. It is normally caught by inhaling infected people's sneezes or after shaking their hands and then touching the face. There is no evidence that being cold and getting caught in the rain in any way causes a person to get a cold; the reason why more people tend to catch colds in winter is because they're often confined to smaller spaces with less ventilation, which are ideal conditions for the propagation of the virus. The best way to prevent a cold is by avoiding others who are infected and frequent hand washing, along with maintaining the body's immune system by eating and sleeping well.

There is no cure for the common cold. The body's immune system eventually kills the virus. Antibiotics are ineffective and any recommended medications – for instance, analgesics such as aspirin and nasal decongestants – work only to alleviate the symptoms; they don't fight the virus. Drinking plenty of fluids also reduces the symptoms of a cold, and vitamin C and zinc tablets are often recommended, but there's no evidence to suggest that they have any positive impact in either preventing or curing a cold, apart from any psychological effects they might have. A common household remedy is chicken soup, which does have some limited effectiveness because it contains cysteine, which is a type of decongestant.

WHAT IS THE INTERNET AND HOW DOES IT DIFFER FROM THE WORLD WIDE WEB?

The terms 'Internet' and the 'World Wide Web' (or just 'Web') are often used interchangeably. However, while they are related, they are actually two completely separate things.

The Internet is a network of networks that links together computers across the world. As long as any two computers are connected to the Internet, they can communicate with each other using a variety of computer languages known as *protocols*. The Internet does not contain information but is the transport vehicle for information stored in documents or files on computers. It's therefore incorrect to say that something is found on the Internet; information is found *using* the Internet, by finding it on a computer that is connected to the Internet.

The Web, invented by Tim Berners-Lee in 1989, is an information-sharing model that is built on top of the Internet. It is a service contained within the Internet and is one of the protocols by which information is thereby provided. When you log on to Microsoft's Internet Explorer, for instance, you're viewing documents on the Web. The Web is one of many Internet applications, and probably the one with which most people are familiar. Another common application used for communication on the Internet is e-mail.

As the Web increased in size, search engines developed to track pages on it and to assist in finding information, the first such being Lycos, which appeared on the scene in 1993. Google is now the largest search engine, tracking over eight billion pages.

WHEN WAS TOILET PAPER INVENTED AND WHAT WAS USED BEFORE THEN?

The Chinese invented toilet paper in the fourteenth century, and the Bureau of Imperial Supplies began to produce paper for use by the Chinese emperors. However, it wasn't until 1857 that the first factory-produced toilet paper was made, by the American Joseph Cayetty, who named his product 'Therapeutic Paper' and sold it in packs of 500 sheets. Cayetty's name was printed on each sheet.

Before the invention of toilet paper, different areas of the world used many different things. Public toilets in ancient Rome provided a moist sponge on the end of a stick, while the wealthy used wool and rosewater.

In Viking-occupied England, discarded wool was used, while in the Middle Ages this had been replaced by hay balls.

In Hawaii, meanwhile, coconut husks were used, while the early Eskimos used snow and tundra moss. Wealthy people around the world often used hemp and wool, with lace being used by the French royalty. British lords used pages from books.

Poorer people used their hands, grass, stones, moss, seashells or wood shavings, while the use of water was also common around the world. In India, the left hand was used to wash with, while in Africa it was the right hand. The other hand in each place was used to greet people, and it was considered rude to offer the incorrect hand.

In the United States, newspapers and telephone directories were commonly used, as were other books. *The Old Farmer's Almanac* was actually printed with a hole punched through the corner of each page so that it could be hung in outhouses, and the Sears catalogue was widely used until it was produced with glossy pages, after which its use as a hygiene product became unpopular. Corncobs were also used in the United States.

WHY DO PEOPLE DREAM?

Dreaming consists of a procession of subconscious

images, thoughts and sounds that we imagine while asleep. Research into dreaming is known as *oneirology*.

It's not known exactly why people dream. In fact, very little is known about dreaming at all, except that it occurs during the rapid eye movement (REM) phase of sleep, when the eyes move rapidly and the brain is highly active. It is also thought that, while most people experience a similar number of dreams, some people simply don't remember their dreams.

Scientists are divided on the function that dreams fulfil. Some believe that they serve a physiological purpose and act to replace the activities of the conscious brain. Such theorists believe that dreams exercise the brain's pathways that are normally used while we are awake, the random impulses that are produced causing our brains to hallucinate in the form of dreaming. Supporting this theory is the fact that it is during our formative years, when the brain and body are growing the most, when most REM sleep and dreams occurs. In addition, scans show that our brainwaves during REM sleep are the same as they are while we're awake but different when we're in deep sleep.

Another school of thought, however, states that dreams serve a psychological purpose and are connected to our emotions and feelings. Proponents of this theory argue that dreams deal with unresolved thoughts and problems that we encounter when we're awake, thereby decreasing the emotional unrest caused by such mental turmoil. The theory is that, if we experience a traumatic event and then dream about it, we will be mentally better prepared for a similar event in the future. Philosophers since Aristotle have shared this view, with later psychologists like Sigmund Freud believing that dreams contain hidden symbolic meanings and insights into our subconscious minds.

Despite such differing views, along with the many books boasting valid interpretations of dreams, most scientists today don't believe that dreams contain any coherent meaning.

HOW SIMILAR ARE HUMANS TO APES?

Whether or not man evolved from apes has been the subject of fierce conjecture for over 100 years. Whatever the real truth, man and ape share a great number of similarities.

Our DNA – the main constituent of chromosomes and the transport medium for our genetic material – is 98.6 per cent the same as that of chimpanzees. While this seems strikingly close, it's worth remembering that many other animals are genetically similar to each other; for example, there's also a 75 per cent similarity between a man and a certain type of worm. Particular genetic parts of dogs are also 90 per cent the same as man, and the haemoglobin of a horse is 88 per cent the same as that of humans. Chimps and gorillas also have forty-eight chromosomes, while humans have forty-six. This seems very close but, taking this to an absurd level, the potato, too, has 46 chromosomes.

Man's appearance is similar to that of apes. Indeed, it has often been said that there isn't a bone or organ in the ape that doesn't have a counterpart in man. However, no bone or organ of an ape would be mistaken for that in a man. While our physical appearance is similar, apes do not constantly walk upright as humans do, nor do they carry weights with their hands. Man also possesses opposable thumbs, which are capable of resisting strain and assist in the operation of tools, while apes do not have these.

The sexual practices of man are, however, very similar to those of chimpanzees, as are many of the characteristics and behavioural patterns of chimps and other apes. However, apes are far less intelligent than man and – except in cases where they are trained by man – exhibit the minimum level of intelligence for survival. Evolutionists claim that our ancestors left the trees and developed an increased brain capacity for dealing with life on the ground. Others, however, reject this.

In his divisive yet groundbreaking 1859 work *On*

the Origin of Species, Charles Darwin postulated a theory of evolution that described how humans and apes had a common ancestor. (It is a common misconception that he wrote that we evolved directly from apes. In fact, he and many others claim that man and ape are divergent strains from a common animal. If this is true, it could explain both the similarities and the differences between man and ape.)

WHO WROTE THE BIBLE, AND WHEN?

The question of who wrote the Bible and when has been debated by scholars for centuries. Most people agree that the current version of the Bible is based on older written sources that have been lost. It is also generally accepted that the Bible is an accurate, factual account of events written in the time that they took place.

A common view is that the Old Testament was written at various times between approximately 1500 BC and 500 BC. The different books are likely to have been written by the different people to whom they are attributed, such as Solomon, Isaiah, Jeremiah, Ezekiel and Daniel. Some books of unknown origin, such as Genesis, Exodus and Leviticus, are thought to have been written by Moses or Ezra the scribe, who studied official records and made books from them.

It is thought that the New Testament was written

between about AD 50 and AD 100. As with the Old Testament, many believe that the different books and chapters of the New Testament were written by those to whom they are attributed, such as Mark, Matthew, John, Luke and Paul, men who are said to have been contemporaries of Jesus.

The men who wrote the Bible came from many walks of life. Peter and John, for instance, were fishermen, while David was the King of Israel and Matthew was a tax collector.

In total, it is thought that over 40 people contributed to the writing of the Bible over a period of about 1,500 years.

WHY DO WOMEN AND NOT MEN TAKE THE CONTRACEPTIVE PILL?

The most common form of female contraception against unwanted pregnancies is known as 'the Pill'. Taken orally on a daily basis, it contains the hormones oestrogen and progesterone, which work to prevent ovulation. The Pill also makes the uterus less likely to accept an embryo, as well as thickening the mucus in the cervix, thus making it more difficult for sperm to reach an egg.

An equivalent male Pill has been in development since the 1960s. This works in a similar way to the female Pill by using synthetic hormones to alter the body's chemical balance in order to stop the production of sperm.

The reason why women take the Pill and not men is because the reproductive system of women is cyclical, regulated by the menstrual cycle, and produces only one egg per month, making women fertile for only about forty-eight hours per month. It was therefore easier for scientists to produce a drug to control this cycle than to control the fertility of men, who produce millions of sperm every day. Producing a drug to control this process, and yet allow it to be reversible later, has proven to be difficult. Under tests, the male Pill caused a high rate of permanent infertility, while other side-effects were kidney and digestive problems, muscle fatigue and paralysis, along with a loss of libido and a decrease in facial hair. To combat this, tests were conducted by introducing the male hormone testosterone into the Pill, which reduced some side-effects but did not stop the infertility problem.

The Chinese ceased their research into the male Pill in 1986, and in 1998 the World Health Organisation recommended that research should be abandoned because of the unacceptable side-effects.

WHERE DOES THE SAYING 'AS MAD AS A HATTER' COME FROM?

The expression 'as mad as a hatter' refers to a person

who is insane or eccentric. It was used famously by Lewis Carroll in his 1865 book *Alice's Adventures in Wonderland*, although he did not coin it. The phrase is also referred to in Thackeray's *Pendennis* of 1849 and Thomas Chandler Haliburton's 1837 book *The Clockmaker*. In fact, the expression existed well before all of these publications.

A hatter was a person who made hats, including felt hats, which were popular in America and Europe. Many of these felt hats were made from rabbit fur. In the early stages of the manufacturing process, the fur was brushed with a mercury-compound solution, which made the fur fibres rougher, enabling them to mat together more easily. The hatters usually worked in areas that were poorly ventilated, causing them to breathe in the mercury compound. After prolonged exposure to the mercury, it accumulated in their bodies, resulting in mercury poisoning, which affected the hatters' nervous systems.

Symptoms of mercury poisoning include tremors and uncontrollable twitches, while in some cases it also caused the hatters' speech to become slurred. Irritability and depression were also common complaints. These symptoms made the hatters appear demented and insane, which gave rise to the expression.

WHY DO PEOPLE HAVE TONSILS?

The tonsils are small clumps of tissue situated on either side of the throat. Nearby but separate to the tonsils are the pharyngeal tonsils, which are also known as the adenoids. An infection of the tonsils is called tonsillitis, which causes the tonsils to become swollen and red, resulting in a fever and sore throat. In severe cases of tonsillitis, swallowing becomes difficult, in which case the tonsils are often removed. This occurs quite frequently and sometimes leads people to ask what the purpose of the tonsils is in the first place.

The tonsils are part of the lymphatic system, and therefore act as part of the immune system, helping the body to fight infection. They contain white blood cells and produce antibodies that fight infections that enter the mouth by food or air, keeping the infection in the throat rather than letting it spread to other parts of the body.

While the tonsils do help to prevent infection, people whose tonsils have been removed are still protected from infection by the other parts of the immune system. It is thought by some that the tonsils' original primary function was to deal with certain types of infection, such as worms or parasites, which are not very common today.

The tonsils are at their largest and most prone to

infection between the ages of three and six; from the age of eight, they begin to shrink and are less likely to become infected. Children also start to increase their resistance to infection as they get older, so any infection of the tonsils becomes increasingly rare as people get older. Also, the antibiotics produced today are very good at fighting infection and reducing inflamed tonsils, making the need to remove the tonsils less common than some years ago.

HOW INTELLIGENT ARE DOLPHINS?

Dolphins are generally considered to be the most intelligent animal in the entire animal kingdom, and the bottle-nose dolphin is thought to be the smartest species of the bunch.

Dolphins are gregarious and social by nature, which is indicative of intelligence. They live in schools and communicate via an intricate array of clicks and whistles, also using ultrasonic sonar to communicate and locate food. They are capable of forming strong bonds with each other.

Dolphins are often comfortable in the presence of humans and have been known to protect humans from shark attacks. They have a high capacity for learning and are capable of extraordinary acrobatic feats in the water. It is thought that they do this in a playful manner, although they can be quickly trained by humans to perform for audiences. Dolphins have also been used in working with disabled children, while military organisations have put them to work in finding mines and rescue operations. They have also been known to guide boats through treacherous reefs.

The size of an animal's brain is often an indication of intelligence. The dolphin's brain is large; in fact, its frontal lobe – the area of the brain thought to relate particularly to intelligence – is larger than that of a human. Their brains also have a highly structured cortex. Dolphins are capable of recognising sign language used by humans and can recognise themselves in a mirror, displaying a level of self-awareness that is very rare in animals and is considered to be a trait of intelligence.

While the testing of the intelligence of dolphins is continuing, it is limited by its expense and the inherent difficulties involved in the testing process.

HOW DO PEOPLE COUNT CARDS IN CASINOS?

Card-counting is a practice that has been occurring in casinos since the 1960s, when books were first published on the topic. Some people, particularly teams of mathematically minded MIT university students, made millions by using card-counting techniques. The practice of card-counting involves the player counting cards to give an advantage over the casino, enabling them to beat the odds and increase their winnings. Many people think that card-counting involves memorising every card that is played so that the next card to be played is definitively known, but this is inaccurate; card-counting is actually the process of remembering how many high-numbered cards have been played in relation to low-numbered cards, which gives the player an indication of the type of cards that are left in the deck.

There have been more than 100 card-counting techniques, although complex systems of card-counting are prone to human error. The most common and successful simple method used is the 'Hi-Lo Count'. In this system, only one number needs to be remembered at any time. 'Plus one' is assigned to cards two, three, four, five and six and 'minus one' is assigned to cards ten, Jack, Queen, King and Ace. 'Zero' is assigned to seven, eight and nine, which are known as neutral cards. The player counts the cards as they are played by adding or subtracting one for each card, depending on its assigned value. An overall positive value means that there is likely to be a greater proportion of high cards in the deck. This gives the player an advantage in Blackjack, for instance – a game in which counting systems are most commonly used – because the dealer is more likely to receive a high card and go bust above twenty-one (the dealer being required by the rules not to sit below seventeen). When the decks are reshuffled, the count begins again from zero.

Card-counting does not help a player to win more hands; it simply means that he or she can alter the size of his or her bet, depending on the count. If the count is low (ie below zero), the player will bet low. If the count is high (generally plus two or more), the player will bet high. In the long run, this should result in the player winning more money than he or she loses.

While card-counting isn't illegal, unless a hidden mechanical device is used, the casino environment makes counting more difficult. The number of decks used per shuffle has increased, the casinos are noisy and full of distractions, and surveillance systems monitor notorious card-counters, who, once spotted, are then removed from or refused entry to casinos.

WHY DO SOME COINS HAVE RIDGES AROUND THE EDGE?

Many years ago, coins were made out of precious metals such as gold and silver. This tempted some people to file flakes of the valuable metals from the edges off the coins and then accumulate the shavings. Some coins, in particular the British sterling-silver coins, were often shaved by opportunist money-handlers to half their minted weight. Merchants were obliged to weigh coins in order to ensure that they were fit and proper, and this of course had an adverse impact on their rate of business. Each incumbent monarch of England during the Tudor Period was forced to recall coins periodically and have them reminted.

To combat this problem, ridges were carved into the edges of the most valuable coins. If the ridges remained unaltered, this showed that none of the precious metal had been shaved off and the coin was still good legal tender. Also, the ridges – collectively known as reeding or milling, while the shapes of the ridges were known as crests and troughs – made counterfeiting more difficult. Only the valuable coins were reeded; lower-denomination coins such as the penny were made of common metal, which made reeding unnecessary, as an opportunistic coin-shaver would need to flake off a huge amount of such metal in order to make his efforts worthwhile.

Today, no coins are made with precious metals, but the tradition of reeding has continued on coins of higher value. In modern times, reeding also helps people who are visually impaired to tell the difference between the various coins, as each is reeded in a different way, while the lower-denomination coins aren't reeded at all. It's therefore possible to distinguish between coins simply by feeling the edge.

DID ROBIN HOOD ACTUALLY EXIST?

The story of Robin Hood has been popularised in numerous books and films over the years. Legend has it that Robin was deprived of his lands by the Sheriff of Nottingham and forced to take refuge in Sherwood Forest, where he became an outlaw, banding with a group of Merry Men, falling in love with a maid named Marian, and stealing from the rich to give to the poor. For many years, people have questioned whether this Good Samaritan really did exist.

The first literary reference to Robin Hood appeared in 1377, where he is portrayed as a common bandit, and there are printed versions of ballads on the subject from the early sixteenth century in which he is portrayed as a farmer or tradesman. In later accounts, it is said that Robin was a nobleman from the late twelfth century, during the time when Richard the Lionheart was fighting the crusades. However, one of the original ballads has it that he lived during the reign of Edward II. While some of the early ballads do refer to the Sheriff of Nottingham and some of the Merry Men, no mention is made of Maid Marian, who is thought to have been added in later versions of the story.

The British Museum keeps an account of Robin's life, which holds that he was born in 1160 in Lockersley, Yorkshire, although this place doesn't exist. Another account, however, has it that he was from Wakefield in the fourteenth century. A tourist attraction in Nottinghamshire is a tree known as the Major Oak, which is said to have been where Robin Hood lived, although this claim has been disputed by some who allege that the tree isn't old enough.

While some academics claim Robin Hood of Sherwood Forest never existed, it is generally accepted that someone referred to as Robin Hood did. Where and when he lived, and how much generosity he bestowed on the poor, remain matters of conjecture, and most experts agree that much of the modern-day legend is just that.

WHAT CAUSES HANGOVERS AND HOW ARE THEY CURED?

A hangover is the after-effect of consuming large amounts of alcohol. The medical term for the condition is *veisalgia*, which means 'uneasiness' and 'pain'. The common symptoms are nausea, headaches, vomiting, diarrhoea, fatigue and anxiety.

While hangovers are caused by a number of factors, the prime culprit is dehydration, a side-effect of the consumption of alcohol, which is a diuretic and therefore causes frequent urination and prevents water reclamation. Because of this, the body's reserves of water become depleted from all organs, including the brain, resulting in headaches. The frequent urination that alcohol consumption promotes also expels the body's salts and potassium, while alcohol breaks down and reduces glucose in the body.

All of the above factors result in weakness and fatigue, but combined with them is the fact that alcohol contains toxins that the body cannot break down when it is consumed in excessive quantities. It also perturbs a person's regenerative sleep patterns, because there is a related increase in the rate of release of the body's natural stimulants once a person has stopped drinking. Also, alcohol consumption results in an elevation in the amount of hydrochloric acid produced in the stomach, which can lead to vomiting or diarrhoea. It's worth noting that dark-coloured drinks tend to retain more toxins from the fermentation process, which can make a hangover worse. Of course, some people are simply more susceptible to hangovers than others, a fact which suggests that genetics plays a role. Psychology, too, is a factor; people who expect to get a hangover have been proven to be more likely to actually get one.

There are many folk remedies for preventing and curing hangovers, but the best way of avoiding – or, at least, reducing – them is to be well rested before drinking and to remain hydrated, with a full stomach, thus slowing down the rate at which the body absorbs the alcohol.

On the day after drinking, a person should continue to keep themselves hydrated, drinking plenty of water, as well as replenishing the body's stores of vitamins B and C by taking multivitamins. Sports drinks can replace lost salts and electrolytes, while drinking fruit juice replaces fructose and helps the body to rid itself of toxins. Bananas, meanwhile, replace lost potassium and eggs provide energy and help the body to break down toxins with the cysteine that they contain. Burned toast is also a proven remedy because of its high levels of carbon, which acts as a filter, attracting and breaking down impurities in the body. Painkillers, meanwhile, can reduce the size of enlarged, headache-forming blood vessels in the brain. Caffeine (another diuretic) should be avoided, however, as should further alcohol – it will only delay the inevitable!

WHERE DID THE TERM 'ROCK 'N' ROLL' COME FROM?

Rock 'n' roll is a globally popular form of fast-paced music combining vocals, electric guitars and strong drum beats. Also known by the abbreviated term 'rock', it originated in the United States in the 1950s.

The words 'rock' and 'roll' were commonly used by African-Americans in the 1920s in reference to partying and drinking, while black people in England used the terms to refer to sex. A number of early songs in the genre written at that time had lyrics containing the words, and by the 1930s the term began to be associated with forms of faster music. In 1934, The Boswell Sisters recorded a song entitled 'Rock And Roll', and by the late 1940s many songs used the words.

In the early 1950s, legendary Cleveland disc jockey Alan Freed was the first to coin the phrase 'rock 'n' roll'. On discovering that rhythm-and-blues records were being bought by white teenagers, he changed the name of his show at the WJW radio station from *Record Rendezvous* to *Moon Dog's Rock 'n' Roll House Party*. He still played the R&B songs on the show, but the inclusion of the term 'rock 'n' roll' meant that any racial association with the music wouldn't dissuade white listeners. In 1954, Freed moved to the WINS station in New York, where he continued playing rock 'n' roll. In that same year, Bill Haley (And His Comets) recorded '(We're Gonna) Rock Around The Clock', which is considered by many to be the first rock 'n' roll song. It was successful throughout the Western world and rock 'n' roll was born.

WHY DO SNOOZE ALARMS GO OFF EVERY NINE MINUTES?

Nearly all digital alarm clocks have a snooze function, which delays the alarm by nine minutes after it has been pressed.

The first snooze alarm clock was an analogue model, created in 1956, and its snooze interval was nine minutes long, which has remained the standard to this day. There are a number of theories as to why this is the standard interval. The most common is that the snooze function is dependent upon the last digit on the clock. In this case, if the snooze delay was ten minutes instead of nine, and the last digit was used, the alarm would go off again immediately following the zero. Proponents of this theory argue that using the last two digits of the clock in the snooze function would involve a more complex design, which might not have been available or feasible at the time when the function was created.

Some experts, meanwhile, say that, when the snooze function was developed, clocks had specific gears. The snooze function, they say, had to fit between two gears, and so, if ten minutes was the desired time delay, the snooze function had to be just under or just over ten minutes.

Of course, others believe that the maker of the first clock selected nine minutes as an arbitrary value that later became the standard that all other alarm clocks have followed ever since.

WHY IS THE US BASEBALL COMPETITION FINAL CALLED THE WORLD SERIES?

At the end of each baseball season in the United States, the winner of the American League competition plays the winner of the National League in a competition known as the World Series. But why, many people ask, is it known as such when it is limited to clubs in North America?

In 1884 the Providence Grays football team beat the New York Metropolitan Club in a three-game series known originally as 'the Championship of the United States', although the press at the time hailed the Grays as 'world champions'. Then the 1887 Spalding Baseball Guide reported on the 1886 post-season series between Chicago and St Louis under the headline 'THE WORLD'S CHAMPIONSHIP', and it was thought that this more impressive name was needed to express the magnitude of the battle between the two US champions. In 1904, the *Reach Guide* dubbed the 1903 Red Sox and Pirates series as the 'World's Championship Series', although by 1912 it had abbreviated this to the 'World's Series' and then, in 1931, to the 'World Series'. The *Spalding Guide* used the term 'World's Series' until 1916, before adopting the now universal term 'World Series' thereafter. This name has remained, despite only teams from the United States and Canada taking part in the competition. Similarly, the winners of the basketball and gridiron competitions in the United States are known as 'world champions'.

Contrary to popular belief, the series was not named after the *New York World* newspaper, which supposedly sponsored the series in the early days. The newspaper has never claimed any association with the World Series, and there is no evidence of sponsorship in any of the editions of the newspaper at the time.

HOW DO PEOPLE PICK LOCKS?

The art of lock-picking is that of opening a lock without using its intended key. There are many different types of locks and a vast array of tools with which to open them. Some combination locks, for example, can be opened by inserting a thin piece of metal between the body of the lock and the shackle, while the locks on car doors can often be opened by sliding a metal ruler between the window and its rubber casing until the ruler hooks under the lock, which can then be lifted up.

The most common type of lock is the *pin-tumbler lock*, which is picked by inserting a device called a *tension wrench* – which can be something as simple as a screwdriver – into the lock. The wrench is then turned slightly, lifting the pins in the lock slightly. Each individual pin is then lifted up into the housing of the lock using a *pick*, which can take the form of any thin, cylindrical piece of metal, such as a hairpin or paper clip. As each pin is lifted, the lock turns fractionally, exposing the next pin to be lifted. (The pins don't all lift up at once because they're not exactly aligned with each other.) Once all of the pins have been lifted, the wrench is used to turn and open the lock.

Another technique to open pin-tumbler locks is known as *raking*, whereby a pick with a wider end is inserted quickly all the way into the lock and then raked back. As it exits, the pick bounces off all of the pins, lifting them in the process, after which the lock is turned with the tension wrench. Raking will often result in a number of the pins being lifted, leaving the remainder to be picked individually. A vibration gun or pick works on the same principle, striking the bottom of all the pins simultaneously while the tension wrench is turned.

Lock-picking is a difficult art to master. The amount of pressure applied must be precise, and the picker must be able to recognise the tiny sounds and vibrations made by the movement of the pins in the lock so that he or she knows when to apply force and, indeed, how much to apply. Acutely tuned senses of touch and hearing are therefore essential.

WHAT IS THE HISTORY OF THE LEANING TOWER OF PISA?

The Leaning Tower of Pisa – originally a *campanile* (bell tower) – is located in the Campo dei Miracoli in the Italian city of Pisa. It measures 55m high and is famous for leaning 4.4m to one side – an inclination of about 10 per cent – when measured from the seventh floor. It's not known for sure who the architect of the tower was, but it's thought to be Bonanno Pisano.

The tower was originally designed to stand vertically but began leaning soon after construction commenced in 1173, as the soil on which it was built was unstable, having once been the sand bed of a river delta. The ground beneath the tower started to sink in 1178 after three storeys had been built. Building was then stopped due to a lack of money and wasn't resumed until 1272, when another four storeys were built and counterweights added to the north side to prevent further leaning. Construction stopped again in 1301 and was eventually completed in 1372, 200 years after it had begun, with the inclusion of the final storey and bell chamber. This bell chamber was originally fully functional and the public were permitted to climb the 296 steps to the top.

A lot of effort has gone into straightening the tower. Mussolini ordered its renovation in the 1930s, and so cement was poured into it, but this only exacerbated the problem and the tower sank further. After other failed attempts, the tower was closed in 1990 due to safety concerns, then underwent stabilisation work and was reopened to the public in 2001.

Legend has it that it was from the Leaning Tower of Pisa that Galileo Galilei famously dropped two cannonballs in order to demonstrate his theory on gravity, although many believe that this experiment occurred elsewhere.

ARE CATS AND DOGS COLOURBLIND?

Historically, it has been thought that both cats and dogs are colourblind. For the last 100 years, extensive tests have been carried out on the colour vision of these animals, generally geared to determining how responsive they are to colours of food. Both animals were found to be unable to distinguish between colours that were signals for food and others that were not, which led scientists to the conclusion that cats and dogs are indeed colourblind.

Evolutionists supported these findings by saying that distinguishing colours wasn't an important survival instinct for dogs or cats, who generally hunt at night and developed heightened senses of smell and hearing to compensate for the deficiency. Recent studies, however, have contradicted these results. Again using experiments with food and colour, it was found that dogs could easily distinguish colours from both extremes of the spectrum (ie reds from blues), as well as being able to differentiate between blues and greens, although they weren't as good at identifying the various colours at the red end of the spectrum. The scientists concluded that dogs aren't colourblind, as was previously believed, but that they suffer from *deuteranopia*, a condition whereby only two of the three types of cones (photoreceptors) in the human retina are present – in the case of dogs, those that pick up blue and red light.

Cats, too, were found to have only blue and red photoreceptors in their retina, indicating that they, like dogs, can see certain colours. Scans of their brains have also indicated that their eyes respond to different wavelengths of light (ie colours), while other studies indicate that cats can learn to distinguish between colours, although this takes a considerable amount of time.

DO HAIR AND FINGERNAILS CONTINUE TO GROW AFTER PEOPLE HAVE DIED?

The claim that hair and fingernails continue to grow

for a period of time after a person dies is a myth. There is often the appearance that this has happened, but it is simply an optical illusion.

When death occurs, all of the cells in the body die, including those that generate hairs and nails, and the body immediately begins to dehydrate. This dehydration causes the skin around a person's hair and fingernails to retract, and it's this receding skin that gives the appearance that the hair and fingernails have grown, whereas in fact they remain the same length; it's the tissues in the skin that have shrunk. People expect hair and fingernails to grow, rather than skin to shrink, and this preconception can support the illusion.

The skin decomposes and shrinks at a faster rate than hair and fingernails, which remain intact for longer and so tend to stand out more prominently. This prominence also leads some people to believe that the hair and fingernails have grown post-mortem. Funeral directors sometimes apply moisturising cream to bodies as a measure to reduce skin shrinkage.

WHY DO PEOPLE CRY?

Crying, or *lachrymation*, is the process of producing tears, which in human eyes are produced by glands under the eyelids. People cry for a number of reasons: basal tears are continually produced to lubricate and clean the eyes, while reflex tears wash away irritants and foreign particles. However, a third type of tears, emotional tears, are produced when a person cries.

When a person is hurt, physically or emotionally, the lachrymal glands sometimes constrict and produce emotional tears. When a person is in an emotionally overwrought state, the body overreacts and produces a flood of hormones and other chemicals found to be present in emotional tears and yet absent in basal and reflex tears. Current thinking has it that crying is beneficial to the body's physical and emotional health, as it helps the body to dispose of these additional stress hormones and chemical toxins and is why people often feel better and calmer after a good cry. Indeed, this view is now supported by scientific research. Even the philosopher Aristotle believed that crying cleansed the mind of suppressed emotions.

Humans are the only animals to cry (although some suggest that gorillas and elephants might, too), largely – it is believed – due to their heightened sense of self-awareness.

CAN BABIES HEAR VOICES WHILE INSIDE THE WOMB?

It has long been suggested that babies can hear voices and music while they are still in the womb, and for years now some mothers have been known to talk to their unborn children and play them music.

A number of studies have now been carried out to test this theory, including one that involved recording sounds picked up by the inner ears of unborn sheep. These studies found that the womb dampens most sounds, except those with low frequencies; high-pitched sounds are muffled. The researchers concluded that deep vowel sounds are likely to be heard but that high-pitched consonants will most likely be inaudible. Music containing a lot of bass is therefore more likely to be heard than classical music.

The researchers further concluded that, while unborn children could probably hear the melody of speech, the definition of individual words would be too muffled to hear. Foetuses younger than thirty weeks were found not to respond to any sounds at all.

The ears of foetuses are filled with water, so they hear via vibrations in their skulls. This makes the mother's voice the most heard sound in the womb, because it vibrates to the baby. This is thought to shape the development of the child to recognise and prefer its native tongue and its mother's voice. It is also believed that babies can recognise music that they heard regularly before they were born. However, no evidence has been found to support the suggestion that certain voices or types of music enhance a child's intelligence.

HOW DO MESSENGER PIGEONS KNOW WHERE TO GO?

Messenger pigeons are actually homing pigeons, a variety of the rock dove that has been selectively bred to be able to navigate its way home. They're not, as is often believed, the same as carrier pigeons, which are kept for ornamental purposes.

For years, messenger pigeons have carried messages written on paper and contained in small tubes, attached to their legs. They were used for such purposes in Baghdad, Persia, in 1150, and in 1850 Paul Reuter – the founder of the investment bank – used them to communicate stock prices between cities. Messenger pigeons were also used extensively during World War I, and indeed they're still used today by remote police departments in India.

The messenger pigeon's ability to deliver messages stems from its love for its home and mate and its desire to return to them. The birds are taken from their homes to their destination and are able to return with messages from hundreds of miles. In some instances, they are made to be familiar with two places, looking to one for food and the other for water. They can then deliver messages between the two places.

It's not known exactly how pigeons are able to find their way home. Some say that they possess a magnetic substance in their brains that enables them to detect the Earth's magnetic lines of force and so can navigate via these lines, while others claim that they use an instinctual form of astronomical navigation. Many others believe, meanwhile, that they have an incredibly strong connection with their homes and are able to return using their senses of smell and hearing.

HOW DO PEOPLE SPEED-READ?

Speed-reading is a well-known method of reading faster than normal. In fact, there are a number of speed-reading techniques, most of which involve visually orientated mental processes as opposed to subvocalisation (ie mentally saying each word in the head without physically uttering it), which slows a reader down. It's estimated that the average subvocaliser reads around 250 words per minute, compared to the 1,000 words per minute read by the average speed-reader.

Speed-readers usually run a finger under each line of text at a fairly fast pace, and while they're learning their craft they often hum a tune to stop them from vocalising the words. This forces them to visualise chunks of text, usually comprising four to five words at a time.

Experienced speed-readers use what is called the *cognitive window*, which involves the brain registering a group of text lines at once and processing the information by the time the finger gets to the end of the text. When a speed-reader's eyes dart back over text that they've read, this action prompts their brain to refresh the cognitive window.

Speed-readers also utilise their context memory, which enables the brain to hold up to seven items of information just read. If they try to remember any more than this, their brains will generally not remember any of them. To combat this, speed-readers group information into four or five concepts at a time. Some visualise a tree shape to organise the concepts into a clear structure, while others imagine giving a PowerPoint presentation with the information they're reading, which forces them to structure the information into coherent groups that don't overload the context memory. Speed-readers also tend to breathe deeply in order to supply the brain with the oxygen it needs to function at the necessary high level of concentration.

Proficient speed-readers argue that comprehension of material read is higher when speed-reading because the brain is not being clogged by sounding out the words. This is disputed by some, however, and most studies have found that speed-readers' comprehension and memory of text aren't as high as those of normal readers.

WAS NOSTRADAMUS ABLE TO PREDICT THE FUTURE?

Michel de Nostredame, commonly known as Nostradamus, lived in France between 1503 and 1566. A well-educated man, he is famous for his book *Les Prophéties*, a compendium of various prophecies that take the form of rhymed four-lined poems called *quatrains*, grouped in sets of centuries. Nostradamus is said to have concocted his prophecies by entering a trance-like state of meditation.

Many believed Nostradamus to possess supernatural powers, and he has been credited with predicting a large number of historical events; indeed, he became famous during his lifetime by supposedly predicting the death of King Henry II of France. People have translated from his writings some other predictions, including those of the atomic bomb, the Great Fire of London, the French Revolution, the discoveries of Louis Pasteur and the atrocities perpetrated by Hitler's Third Reich.

One of Nostradamus's most famous predictions was that a great disaster would occur in July 1999 – a disaster that, in fact, did not happen. In the typical style of his prophecies, it read, 'In the year 1999 and seven months, a great King of Terror will come from the sky./He will bring back the great king Genghis Khan, before and after Mars rules happily.' It is also said by some that he predicted the 9/11 terrorist attacks in the prophecy that reads, 'At forty-five degrees, the sky will burn./Fire approaches the great new city./Immediately a huge scattered flame leaps up,/When they want to have verification from the Normans.' In fact, New York City is below the forty-first parallel but, as often happens with Nostradamus's prophecies, this quatrain was misquoted to make it more relevant to 9/11 and then circulated on the Internet.

Sceptics claim that Nostradamus's prophecies are written in an intentionally ambiguous manner and are sufficiently vague as to be capable of being applied to many events, while the prophecies are further obscured by often being written in a mixture of languages. Critics also argue that the prophecies have always been interpreted with the benefit of hindsight in what is called 'retroactive clairvoyance'. None of the prophecies has been interpreted before a specific event.

WHAT IS SUBLIMINAL ADVERTISING AND DOES IT WORK?

Subliminal advertising is the practice of briefly inserting a signal or message into an advertisement with the intention of that message then being perceived directly by the subconscious mind of the recipient while being imperceptible to his or her conscious mind. Such an artifice is designed to appeal to the subconscious mind and strongly influence people's behaviour in order to compel them to purchase products. One example is hidden pictures that are flashed up so fast that they aren't detected by the conscious mind but the subconscious mind registers them. Sounds that are inaudible to the conscious mind can also be used as subliminal messages, while it's said that lyrics to songs that are played backwards to give a different meaning are another form of subliminal communication.

Proponents of subliminal advertising claim that the signals are not recognised or screened by the critical conscious mind, making them more powerful than normal messages that the recipient can disregard.

Subliminal advertising came to the fore in the United States in the 1950s, when a number of books were published claiming its existence and provoked a public outcry. One researcher described the results of a 1957 experiment where the words 'Drink Coca-Cola' and 'Hungry? Eat Popcorn' were flashed on a New Jersey movie screen over a six-week period. He claimed that popcorn sales rose by 57.8 per cent over the next six weeks and Coke sales rose by 18.1 per cent. Largely as a result of this experiment, subliminal advertising was banned in America in

1958, although the researcher later admitted to falsifying his results.

Despite popular belief, there is little evidence to support that subliminal advertising has ever existed. Even if it has, most experts agree that there is nothing to suggest that it in any way influences the thoughts or actions of the recipient.

HOW DO SALMON FIND THEIR EXACT BIRTHPLACE?

Once salmon are born, they remain in their native stream for up to three years before swimming to the ocean, where they live for two to three years until they reach maturity. During this time, they travel thousands of miles before returning to their native stream to spawn the next generation. They pass by numerous suitable rivers on their way to spawn and yet always manage to make it to the river in which they were born. All of their energy is deployed in completing this act and, once they have spawned, they die. It is one of nature's most remarkable phenomena.

The process by which salmon are able to find their exact birthplace has been researched for years. Most scientists agree that the ability of the salmon to find their native stream is not inherited and must be learned. Some believe that salmon navigate using the Earth's magnetic field as a compass, while others think that they use the sun and moon as directional aids. One possible explanation might be found in the lateral line that salmon have on the sides of their bodies, which helps them to detect very small shifts in water currents and might also serve as a direction finder.

Salmon also have an incredibly acute sense of smell and are thought to be able to detect a single differentiating drop of liquid in over 250 gallons of water. Scientists believe that salmon can remember the distinctive smell of their native stream from the time when they lived there, and that, once the fish have navigated to within range of their native stream, they use this powerful sense of smell to direct them to it. Many experts believe that the smell that salmon trace is from a unique blend of vegetation, insects and dust from the rocks and soil in the native stream giving each stream a unique composition that the salmon are able to remember.

Others believe that the salmon's ability to smell its native stream is triggered by pheromones that are released into the ocean by other salmon from the same stream. The salmon then homes in on the smell of these pheromones, allowing it to guide it to its native stream.

WHY DOES THE DATE FOR EASTER CHANGE?

Easter is a religious holiday based on the resurrection of Jesus, the exact date of which was not recorded. In light of this, no generally accepted date for Easter was fixed, and the date was based on the calendar.

However, the decision of which calendar to use was a point of contention. The Julian calendar was the solar-based calendar of the Roman Empire since 45 BC, but the Lunar calendar (which was Jewish) had been in place for 2,000 years before that. Because of the differences in the calendars, Easter was celebrated on different dates. In AD 325, a conclave of priests and bishops met at Christianity's first Ecumenical Council in Nicea (present-day Turkey) to decide an array of topics, one of which was the date for Easter. The different Church groups were represented and a decision was eventually reached. It was decided that, throughout the Church, Easter would be celebrated on the first Sunday after the first full moon that occurs on or after 21 March. Different regions, however, applied slightly different rules, some describing 21 March as the Vernal Equinox (ie the Spring Equinox, when the length of night and day are equal because the sun passes over the equator), although the first Sunday after the first full moon that occurs on or after 21 March is now the accepted formula.

Applying this formula, Easter Sunday must fall between 22 March and 25 April, inclusive. Easter Sunday hasn't fallen on 22 March since 1818 and will next fall on that date in 2285. Similarly, it hasn't fallen on 25 April since 1943 and won't again until 2038.

WHAT IS THE ORIGIN OF THE TERM 'RULE OF THUMB'?

In recorded use as early as 1692, the term 'rule of thumb' is an expression that describes using the thumb as a rough means for testing or measurement. Its precise origin is unknown.

One school of thought has it that, across the ages, people such as carpenters and seamstresses have used the thumb as a measuring guide. The expression has also been linked to brewers, who allegedly used their thumb as a temperature gauge before the advent of the thermometer.

Using body parts was an ancient means of calculating measurement – for example, the height of a horse was measured in hands and the modern units of feet and yards were originally determined by the length of an adult pace. Similarly, it has been suggested that the measurement of an inch was derived from the distance between the thumb's first joint and its tip.

However, there is another, more controversial,

etymology of the saying. Some claim that the expression is derived from the maximum size of the stick with which a husband was permitted to beat his wife – ie as long as the stick was no thicker than the man's thumb, it was lawful practice. There has been much argument over whether this 'rule of thumb' was ever enshrined in law. Proponents of the theory that it was a doctrine of English common law cite that, in 1782, Justice Francis Buller made mention of the rule in one of his judgments, arguing further that there have also been various references made to the rule in United States' court decisions in the nineteenth century. People who disagree with this theory claim that nothing concerning such a 'law' was ever formally laid down in legislation.

The exact origin of the phrase is a matter of conjecture and is likely never to be certain.

WHAT IS THE SMALL THING THAT HANGS AT THE BACK OF THE MOUTH?

The small piece of flesh that hangs down at the back of the human mouth is called the *uvula* (pronounced 'yoovyoolla') and is found at the junction of the palate and the throat. Its medical name derives from the Latin word for 'grape' because of its shape, which tends to be that of a small cylinder not dissimilar to a grape. It's sometimes split in two, but this is unusual.

Often mistaken for the epiglottis (the flap of skin that covers the windpipe when people swallow), the uvula's function is to assist in the creation of certain sounds for the human voice. In conjunction with the throat, it varies the direction of air from the lungs to form an array of sounds. However, it can also be vibrated during sleep, and this can contribute to people snoring. In extreme cases – especially where it is larger than normal – it can be removed.

While the uvula can become infected and enlarged, causing breathing difficulties, this occurs infrequently. Generally speaking, the uvula causes little trouble.

HOW DO RABBITS AND HARES DIFFER?

Rabbits and hares are often confused and yet are completely different animals, with a number of distinguishing attributes. To add to the confusion, hares are sometimes known as 'jack rabbits'.

Despite their similarities in appearance, the two animals are from different species. The differences between the two start from birth. Hares are born fully furred, able to move and see, whereas rabbits are hairless, blind and helpless. For this reason, the rabbit is closely cared for by its mother in a nest while the hare is left to fend for itself.

Physically, hares are much larger than rabbits, with

much bigger ears and stronger hind legs, making it a faster runner than the rabbit and with higher endurance, often being able to outrun its enemies. The fur of a hare also changes to a lighter colour in winter, while the rabbit's pelt maintains its colour throughout the year. Unlike those of the rabbit, the hare's ears are black-tipped, while the skulls of the two animals also vary slightly.

Rabbits live in colonies in burrows tunnelled in the ground, where male rabbits fight for dominance. Hares, however, are solitary creatures that seldom fight and come together only for mating. They don't make burrows, preferring to live on the land among vegetation.

Other differences can be found in the animals' diets, where the rabbit eats fresh grass or vegetables while the hare eats harder food, such as bark and twigs. The flesh of the rabbit is also light, similar to that of a chicken, whereas the hare's flesh is darker and reddish.

Apart from their similarities of shape and the way in which they hop, rabbits and hares really are completely different animals.

HOW DID THE GAME OF RUGBY ORIGINATE?

It's commonly believed that the game of rugby was

born in 1823 at Rugby School in England, where during a game of soccer a student named William Webb Ellis, frustrated with the rules, allegedly picked up the ball and ran with it. Despite there being little evidence to support this popular view, the winner of the modern Rugby World Cup is presented with the William Webb Ellis trophy and Rugby School has a plaque commemorating the incident.

However, many argue that the game existed in one form or another for hundreds of years before 1823. It's said that the sixth-century Roman sport of *harpastum*, originating in China, was an origin for rugby, while other regions also had sports that involved having the ball in the hand. The Irish, for instance, played *caid* (the word meaning 'bull's scrotum', presumably because the ball was made from one), the Welsh had *criapan* and the Vikings had *knappan*. Rugby might have had its roots in any one or even all of these games.

Despite the potential influence of these early games, there is little doubt that William Webb Ellis's act was instrumental in the beginnings of organised rugby and a definitive moment in the formation of the modern game. By 1838, with the added contribution of a strong runner named Jem Mackie, running with the ball was an acceptable part of the game and was made a legal part of the game in 1841. The first rules were written by students of Rugby School in 1845.

The first rugby balls, meanwhile, were fashioned by a boot and shoemaker in Rugby named William Gilbert (1799–1877), who began making balls for Rugby School out of pigs' bladders encased in leather. Indeed, the Gilbert company still exists today, and the modern-day rugby ball bears its name. The ball's oval shape is said to derive from the shape of the pigs' bladders used many years ago.

In 1871, the Rugby Football Union was formed by a committee in Regent Street, London, where three former pupils of Rugby School wrote formal rules for the game. Then, in 1886, the International Rugby Board was formed. Rugby is now one of the most popular international sports.

WHERE DID THE NAME 'KU KLUX KLAN' ORIGINATE?

The Ku Klux Klan was a secret organisation of white supremacists formed in the United States in 1865 by ex-members of the Confederate Army. This group was disbanded in 1880 and a second group, using the same name and preaching racism, formed in 1915. The prominence of this group was reduced during the Great Depression in the 1930s, but it resurfaced again in the '50s and '60 s in opposition to the Civil Rights movement.

The name is sometimes incorrectly referred to as

'the Klu Klux Klan', often abbreviated to 'the KKK'. The unusual first two words of the name, 'Ku Klux', are said to be a variation of the Greek word *kuklos*, which means 'circle', chosen supposedly because it is a symbol of unity, perfection and secrecy. 'Klan', meanwhile, is said to be an obvious variation of the word 'clan', with the K being substituted to make the name alliterative.

Another theory suggests that the name was selected because the three Ks sound like the cocking of a gun. Members of the KKK have rejected this, however, and it seems likely that the Greek origin is correct.

WHAT IS THE DIFFERENCE BETWEEN AN OCEAN AND A SEA?

All of the oceans and seas on the planet are part of one continuous body of water, which, because of its size, has been divided up into various parts. Seas are smaller than oceans and are sometimes partially land-locked. They are often extensions of oceans and indent from an ocean into a landmass. Once the sea moves away from the landmass, it becomes the ocean. Other than those distinctions, oceans and seas do not differ and the terms are often used interchangeably.

In the early days, explorers often used the term 'the seven seas', by which they referred to the Red Sea,

Mediterranean Sea, East African Sea, West African Sea, China Sea, Indian Ocean and Persian Gulf. In the present-day system of nomenclature, there are five oceans – the Pacific (sometimes split into North and South Pacific), Arctic, Indian, Atlantic (also often split into North and South oceans) and Antarctic – along with many more seas. Today, each sea under the current definition is linked to an ocean so that water from one of the oceans can flow into the sea. One exemption to this rule is the Caspian Sea, which is completely enclosed by land and is often thought of as a lake.

Whether bodies of water are called seas, oceans, gulfs or bays is often simply a result of when and by whom they were named.

WHY IS NEW YORK CITY CALLED 'THE BIG APPLE'?

The origin of New York City's most famous nickname has been the subject of conjecture for many years. One view is that one New York gentleman's guidebook to the houses of ill repute in the nineteenth century referred to New York as having the best 'apples' (in this usage, a euphemism for prostitutes) in the world. Given that New York claimed to have the most and best brothels, it was inevitably called 'the Big Apple'. A second view is that the name was derived from a 1909 book by Edward S Martin entitled *The Wayfarer In New York*, which made a reference to New York being the big apple and receiving more than its share of the 'national sap'. However, there is no evidence to suggest that either of these two sources had any influence on the popularity or spread of the term.

Many people believe that the name stems from a term used by jazz musicians to refer to New York, although it is thought that they did not begin the trend. That honour is believed to fall to John Fitzgerald, a horseracing journalist for the *New York Morning Telegraph*, who in 1921 wrote an article in which he referred to New York races around 'the Big Apple'. Fitzgerald claimed that he overheard the term being used by some African-American stablehands in New Orleans, who referred to every jockey's dream being to race in New York because 'there's only one Big Apple. That's New York.' The name was then popularised by jazz musicians in the 1930s because New York – and, in particular, Harlem – was the best place to perform and thought to be the jazz capital of the world.

In 1971, a New York advertising campaign adopted the name 'The Big Apple' (using a logo featuring red apples) in an attempt to increase tourism to the city by portraying it as a bright and lively place rather than an urban netherworld rife with crime. Since then, the city has officially been known as the Big Apple throughout the world. In 1997, the corner of Fifty-fourth Street and Broadway, where John Fitzgerald lived for twenty-nine years, was named Big Apple Corner as a tribute to the man.

WHY DO MEN AND WOMEN GAIN WEIGHT IN DIFFERENT PARTS OF THE BODY?

Most people are aware that men tend to accumulate fat on their bellies while on women it usually accumulates on their thighs, hips and bottoms. This is actually because of genetic and hormonal differences between men and women.

The fat on a pot-bellied man is located deep in the abdomen area, around the internal organs, including the stomach muscles, which is why the abdomens of large men are still often very hard. While this fat presents a health risk, it is generally easily lost.

On the other hand, the fat on a woman's lower body poses less of a health risk because it contains a particular enzyme that takes harmful lipids out of the bloodstream, causing women to store the fat easily in these areas. Unfortunately, this also makes it more difficult to lose.

It is thought by some that the fat is stored in these different areas on men and women so that it is kept away from and therefore harmless to the sexual organs. A man's abdomen is removed from his testicles, whereas a woman's abdomen surrounds her uterus, and so the fat is stored on her hips and thighs, which are further away.

There is another theory concerning why the different genders store fat differently this way, but this one is rooted in the process of evolution. In the time of our early ancestors, men hunted wild animals while women gathered fruit, berries and seeds. It was therefore important for men to be able to chase prey in order to feed their families. Excess weight was not conducive to this. However, a man's centre of gravity is located behind the abdominal muscles, so, if weight is to be stored anywhere, that's the most advantageous place, as it won't hinder him too much and he will still be able to run efficiently. Women didn't need to run, so it wasn't as much of an evolutionary necessity for them to store fat near their centres of gravity. In fact, it was important for women not to have large stomachs, which could give the impression that they were pregnant, a fact that was likely to deter male suitors, whose instincts were to seek a receptive mate.

WHAT MAKES A VALUABLE DIAMOND?

The more rare and beautiful a diamond is, the more valuable it is. A diamond's rarity and beauty are based on what are known as the four Cs: colour, clarity, carat and cut.

A fine diamond should be colourless. While most people see all diamonds as being colourless, many often contain impurities that show up as traces of yellow or grey. Pure diamonds – which are the most valuable – are colourless and are graded 'D' while yellowy diamonds are graded 'Z'.

It's generally held that the greater a diamond's clarity – ie the greater the extent to which it is free from blemishes (imperfections on the surface of the diamond, which reduce its value) and inclusions (minerals or fractures, generally very difficult to see with the naked eye, that appear while the diamond is being formed) – the more beautiful it is, and certainly D-grade diamonds are rarer than Z-grade stones.

A diamond's carat rating relates to its weight. One carat is about 0.2g. The larger the diamond is, the rarer it is and the more each additional carat is worth. There are 100 points in a metric carat, so a diamond of 50ct weighs half a carat. Diamonds that are larger than one carat are considered rare and are generally very valuable.

The cut of a diamond is man's only influence on a diamond's beauty and value and has a direct effect on the way in which it reflects light and sparkles. A diamond that is well cut will reflect light internally until it comes through the top of the diamond, while a diamond that is cut too deeply or too shallowly will lose the reflected light through its base or side. A well-cut diamond therefore appears more brilliant, and this makes it more valuable. The most rare and expensive diamonds, of course, exhibit each of the above qualities.

WHY DO WHALES BEACH THEMSELVES?

The phenomenon of whales beaching themselves, either singly or in large groups, has long been a scientific mystery. Sometimes beached whales – especially large ones – are already dead and simply wash up on shore, although in many cases beached whales are alive. The reason for this behaviour is still unclear. When beached, whales often die of dehydration, drown when high tides cover their blowholes or suffocate under their own weight.

The species of whales that beach themselves alive swim in large herds. Pilot whales, which have a tendency to strand themselves *en masse*, have a complex social structure and exhibit extreme loyalty to members of the group that are in trouble. It is thought that, if the lead pilot whale becomes disoriented or sick, and unable to keep itself at the surface to breathe, it might swim ashore. The rest of the group will then follow it as a response to its distress call, or out of loyalty, only to suffer the same fate.

It is also believed that whales use the Earth's magnetic field, combined with an awareness of coastal topography, to navigate. In places where these factors are abnormal, whales might become disoriented and think that the water is deeper than it is. Lending weight to this theory is the fact that whales are often found stranded in the same place and, if towed back into the water, typically strand themselves again on the same beach.

Whales are often found stranded where the beach slopes away gradually, which has led some to believe that, in such places, the sonar system used by whales to measure distance has nothing to bounce back from, giving the whale the impression that deep water lies ahead. Others believe that whales chase their prey into shallow waters before getting stranded by the ebbing tide.

Another theory is that underwater sonar used by navies and noises emitted during seismic testing for oil and gas are so intense that whales are forced to surface too quickly. The resulting rapid change in pressure can cause decompression sickness or haemorrhaging in their ears, which can confuse them or inhibit their navigational abilities, causing them to become beached.

WHY IS BELLY-BUTTON LINT GENERALLY BLUE?

A number of surveys have been undertaken in relation to belly-button lint. They have all found that the lint is generally blue in colour and is more prevalent in the navels of certain types of people. To answer why it tends to be blue, the origin of the lint must first be considered.

It's thought that the lint comprises fibres from clothing, as well as some skin cells, that are channelled to the navel from below by hairs on the stomach throughout the day as the body moves. These hairs also help to dislodge the fibres from the clothes.

Generally speaking, the stomach hairs are particularly important in this process, which is why hairy men tend to accumulate the most lint. Similarly, older (and, therefore, hairier) people also often acquire more lint, while shaving the stomach has been found to reduce navel-lint build-up.

It has also been found that men with large stomachs accumulate more lint, probably because their abdomens press harder against their clothing, causing more fibres to dislodge, and also because their navels tend to be deeper, allowing more lint to accumulate there. The reason why the lint stays in the navel is either because the navel contains perspiration that the lint clings to (as some suggest) or because the lint simply lodges there because the navel is set lower than its surroundings. Supporting this theory is the fact that outward-protruding navels rarely collect lint.

The reason why the lint is coloured blue has been the subject of much conjecture, but it's generally thought to be related to the colour of the clothing worn below the navel, which is generally dark colours such as blue. However, the lint of people who wear a variety of colours still tends to be blue, because blue is the result of combining a number of different colours, just as the lint found in the filters of washing and drying machines tends to be bluish in colour, being a combination of the fibres from all of the clothes in the load.

WHY DO PHONE NUMBERS IN AMERICAN MOVIES ALL START WITH 555?

Phone numbers in American movies and television shows usually begin with the fictional prefix 555. The reason why a fictional prefix was chosen for all onscreen phone calls is one of privacy. A few decades ago, the first letters of exchange names were used as part of telephone numbers in America, followed by numbers. The number five on the dial corresponded with the letters J, K and L, but no exchange-name abbreviation could be made with any combination of these three letters. Instead, the

555 prefix was allocated to service providers' numbers, such as the directory assistance number, which is 555 1212. Anyone attempting to call a number used in a movie or television show would therefore be able to contact only a service provider, not a registered phone customer, which removed the potential for viewers to harass other customers. (There have been instances where 555 numbers were not used on television and a multitude of crank calls have been made to the number.)

In order to stop any further confusion from disrupting service providers, the numbers 555 0100 to 555 0199 are now specifically reserved for fictional use.

WHY DOES COFFEE KEEP YOU AWAKE?

As almost everyone knows, coffee keeps you awake because it contains caffeine, a drug that produces a number of chemical reactions in the brain that act to keep you awake.

Caffeine works by blocking the brain's ability to absorb adenosine, which slows down nerve activity, causing the human body to become sleepy. A caffeine molecule is chemically similar to adenosine but, when it attaches itself to a nerve cell, it doesn't cause the cell to slow down but instead blocks the nerve's adenosine receptor, which in turn causes an increase in the nerve cell's level of activity. This increase causes the body to think something is wrong and it goes into 'flight or fight' mode. As a result, the body floods the bloodstream with adrenalin, which increases blood pressure and heart rate. It also increases the rate of blood flow to the muscles and dilates the alveoli and bronchioles in the lungs, all of which keep the human body awake.

In the same way that amphetamines do, caffeine also increases the body's levels of dopamine, a neurotransmitter that stimulates brain function and induces an overall sense of wellbeing, making you feel more energetic.

While the effects of caffeine consumption are brief, continuous intake over longer periods can lead to an increased level of tolerance. If this happens, when a person then doesn't have caffeine, the body can become oversensitive to adenosine, which in turn can lead to a drop in blood pressure and resultant headaches, irritability and deficiency in regenerative deep sleep. Prolonged excessive usage of caffeine can lead to addiction and intoxication.

HOW DID THE MARATHON RACE BEGIN?

The marathon is an athletics event that gets its name from the Greek town of Marathon, where a Persian army landed in 490 BC, seeking to conquer Greece.

Against the odds, the Greeks defeated the Persians, and legend has it that a young Greek man named Pheidippides ran from the battlefield at Marathon to Athens to give word of the victory. It is also said that he died shortly after the run.

No evidence has ever been found to suggest that Pheidippides ever ran to Athens. In fact, it is suggested that he ran from Athens to Sparta in an attempt to seek support for the battle. However, many later accounts include mention of the alleged incident and the legend continued.

It is estimated that the distance between the battlefield at Marathon and Athens is 34.5km, but the length of the modern race was not initially regimented and varied from course to course.

The marathon was included in the first modern Olympics in 1896 on the suggestion of a man named Michel Bréal, who was fascinated with the legend of Pheidippides and wanted to include a long-distance race to commemorate the competition. This was supported by the Greeks and by Pierre de Coubertin, the French baron who founded the modern Olympics, and was eventually included as the final event of the Games.

At the 1908 Olympics in London, the distance of the course from Windsor Castle was 42.195km. The distances of later Olympic marathons varied until

1921, when the distance of the 1908 London marathon – 26 miles and 385 yards – was set as the official length for the race.

WHY DO BOTTLES OF TEQUILA CONTAIN WORMS?

It's a common misconception that tequila bottles contain worms; indeed, it is legally forbidden for bottles of tequila to contain worms. In fact, it is the drink mezcal – similar to tequila and also made in Mexico – that contains the worm. A number of brands of mezcal contain worms.

The worm traditionally used for such a purpose is actually the caterpillar *Hipopta agavis*, which lives in the stems of agave plants, from which mezcal is made. These reddish-coloured worms can be quite rare and at times white worms from the leaves of the plant are used instead.

The practice of adding such worms to bottles of mezcal has been in existence since the 1940s, when a Mexican named Jacobo Lozano Paez, while tasting the drink, found that the addition of the worm changed the taste and colour. He then decided to include the worm as a marketing gimmick. Despite popular belief, this practice hasn't been a Mexican tradition for centuries.

The worm is supposed to be eaten, traditionally

being considered a delicacy by Mexicans, and is thought by some to have aphrodisiac qualities, while others believe that the worm gives strength to those who eat it and that it is an hallucinogenic. Apart from any psychological effects the worm might have, however, in reality it's merely a worm filled with alcohol.

WHAT ARE APHRODISIACS AND DO THEY WORK?

Aphrodisiacs are substances that are thought to stimulate sexual excitement when consumed. Indeed, the term *aphrodisiac* is derived from the Greek goddess of love and beauty, Aphrodite.

Many aphrodisiacs were classed as such through the ancient belief that they would work if they resembled the genitalia – for example, two common aphrodisiacs, rhino horn and oysters, are supposed to resemble male and female genitalia, respectively. Tiger bones are also thought to be aphrodisiacs (because of the power of the animal), as are bulls' testicles. Chocolate, however, is not technically an aphrodisiac, although a chemical present in it – phenylethylamine – is thought by some to increase arousal. Alcohol and certain other drugs, such as ecstasy, also reduce inhibitions and make people feel more aroused, but they too are not technically aphrodisiacs.

There is no medical evidence that the consumption of so-called 'aphrodisiacs' actually increases sexual arousal, or that they contain anything that has this effect. Scientists believe that aphrodisiacs exist only in myth and folklore, passed down through the ages.

While they have no proven physical impact, however, it is thought by some that substances held to have aphrodisiac qualities might produce a sufficiently strong psychological effect to increase a person's state of arousal, possibly because the person expects to become aroused and this expectation then leads to arousal.

WHY DOES CATNIP AFFECT CATS?

Catnip is the common name for the many species of nepeta, a weed-like herb from the mint family, *Lamiaceae*. Its common name derives from the fact that, when domestic cats are exposed to its smell, they often behave in a peculiar manner.

Catnip affects different cats in different ways, but the most common reaction is for the cat to enter a state of blissful excitement. It will purr and salivate, often sniffing, licking or eating the plant. It might also roll around in the catnip and rub against it. The reaction tends to last a few minutes, after which the cat will withdraw, before sometimes returning a few hours later. The herb has been known to affect cats on their first encounter with it, although kittens and older cats often have no reaction. It is also thought to affect big cats, such as lions, leopards and tigers.

It is not known exactly why cats, and only cats, react in this unusual way. However, it is known that catnip contains a chemical compound called *nepetalactone*, which is contained in part as an oil in the leaves of the plant and is thought to stimulate cats through their sense of smell, increasing their heart rates. It is speculated that catnip has a narcotic affect on cats, which might cause them to hallucinate. Others believe that nepetalactone acts as an aphrodisiac, stimulating cats sexually due to the fact that it is similar to a chemical contained in the urine of female cats – which itself might explain why some species of catnip smell like cat urine and why neutered male cats generally react less vehemently to catnip.

Research also suggests that, while a cat's susceptibility to the effects of catnip is inherited, catnip is not addictive and is completely harmless.

WHY IS FRIDAY THE 13TH THOUGHT TO BE UNLUCKY?

It is a common superstition in Western society that the thirteenth day of any month is unlucky if it falls on a Friday. An irrationally morbid fear of such a date is known as paraskevidekatriaphobia (triskaidekaph-obia being that of the number thirteen), deriving from the Greek words *paraskevi* (Friday), *dekatria* (thirteen) and *phobos* (fear).

There is an array of explanations for the origin of the superstition. For instance, it was on Friday, 13 October 1307 that the Grand Master of the Knights Templar and his senior knights were arrested by the king of France, tortured and killed, while another suggestion has it that it originated from Scandinavia, where twelve feasting gods were joined by Loki, an evil god, and as a result of his actions misfortune occurred on Earth. Meanwhile, a common Christian belief of its origins derives from the Last Supper in the Bible, where the traitor Judas was the thirteenth disciple and Jesus was executed on a Friday.

Despite the origins of the superstition, there is existing evidence suggesting that the date is actually unlucky for some people. Studies have shown that a greater number of car accidents and other sorts of mishaps happen on Friday the 13th than on other Fridays. However, psychologists think that this might be a result of people having an increased sense of anxiety because of the date.

The date also has an effect on society as a whole. For example, it is thought that many people do not travel to work on Friday the 13th because of their fear, while many of the world's office buildings contain no floor thirteen. It is also considered by many to be unlucky for thirteen people to have dinner together.

As mentioned earlier, however, fear of Friday the 13th is a purely Western phenomenon; certain other cultures consider alternate dates to be unlucky.

HOW DO MIRRORS WORK?

A mirror is a simple device whose operation is based on a phenomenon known as *reflection*, which dictates that, when particles of light – known as *photons* – hit the surfaces of certain objects, they bounce off at the same angle at which they hit. By this scientific principle, because a mirror has a smooth surface, it reflects back a coherent reflection of the image in front of it as photons rebound off its surface. (Rough surfaces don't reflect because the photons bounce off in many directions and become scattered.) Obviously, not all smooth surfaces reflect like mirrors. This is because some surfaces absorb the photons and do not reflect them.

To prevent light from being absorbed and to aid in reflection, the glass in most household mirrors has a thin layer of smooth aluminium applied to the rear side to create what's known as a *back-silvered mirror*. This layer of aluminium reflects the light through the clear glass to produce a 'mirror image' of the object in front of it. Meanwhile, the rear side of the aluminium is usually painted black in order to seal and protect the aluminium coating, which provides the reflection. It is thought that such mirrors reflect approximately 80 per cent of the photons that hit them.

On a one-way mirror (sometimes erroneously called a two-way mirror), the film of metal applied to the glass is very thin and so it reflects about half the photons that hit it and lets the other half pass through it. When used between a bright room and a dark room, such a mirror reflects the light in the bright room and seems transparent in the darker room.

HOW DID THE WORD 'SHIT' ORIGINATE?

It is claimed by some that the word *shit* originates in the sixteenth century, when manure was transported by ship. The dry manure weighed little and was stowed below deck. When mixed with water, however, it gained in weight and began to ferment, producing methane gas, which, when exposed to a naked flame (that of a lantern, for instance), would ignite, causing explosions and fires. Because of these accidents, crates of manure were labelled 'Ship High In Transit' to indicate that the crates were to be stowed above the deck, so that any water that the ship took on would not come into contact with them. It was assumed by many that the word *shit* was an acronym derived from this labelling convention. However, this theory has since been discovered to be a complete falsehood that can be traced to an Internet posting in 1999 and that has been perpetuated ever since.

The word *shit* is from the Middle English word *shitten*, which in turn derived from the Old English word *scitan*, from *besciten*, which meant 'to be covered with excrement' and is in turn thought to originate from the Indo-European root *skei*. The word can also be traced back to Germanic languages at the time of the Roman Empire. The word *shite*, meanwhile, is a variant form of the word that is found in some dialects in Ireland and Scotland, as well as in colloquial English.

HOW CAN YOU TELL IF SOMEONE IS LYING?

There are various classic signs and signals to look for in order to decipher whether someone is lying to you. Generally speaking, a person cannot fake their own body language, so you should look for inconsistencies between what is being said and the person's gestures. For this, you must be vigilant and alert.

If a person touches their face or nose when they are talking, it can indicate that they are attempting to hide the words, suggesting in turn that they are lying. Similarly, the crossing of the arms or legs is a defensive gesture that liars sometimes subconsciously employ. Tightening of the lips and clenching of the jaw are also nervous signals of a liar, as is fidgeting restlessly with the fingers. A lot of stuttering while talking and the use of 'um' and 'ah' can indicate a liar, as can talking uncharacteristically quickly, which might stem from the liar's wish to say the lie quickly in order to get it over with.

Probably the most telling feature to watch in a suspected liar is their eyes. If a person is unwilling to look you in the eyes when they talk but their eyes dart around the place, this might suggest that they are lying. Excessively pronounced eye contact can also indicate a liar, as if the liar is trying desperately to appear credible. However, a more compelling indication is if a person looks to the sky while talking, which can indicate that they are trying to access either the visual (remembering something that happened) or creative (to fabricate something) area of the brain. These areas are accessed differently by left- and right-handed people. When a right-handed person looks up and to the right, for instance, the creative area of the brain is being accessed and a lie is most likely being told, while a left-handed person would look up and to the left.

An increased rate of blinking can also flag a lie being told, as the stress of telling a lie can cause parts of the body – for example, the eyes – to become dry, compelling an increased rate of blinking. Similarly, the licking of dry lips can indicate that a lie is being told.

Another method of lie detection, which is thought to be accurate, is to look for facial microexpressions. When a person lies, their forehead or the area between their eyes creases slightly to indicate distress. However, these facial movements are almost imperceptible to the untrained eye.

WHY DO MEN FEEL SLEEPY AFTER SEX?

It has long been a common complaint of women that men fall asleep straight after sex. Men do, indeed, suffer post-coital lethargy, but there is a physiological explanation for it.

While some studies have concluded that sex has no impact on how tired a man feels, it is now believed that sex has a tendency to induce sleep in men because of the impact it has on certain chemicals in the brain.

Just prior to ejaculation, the brain produces high quantities of dopamine, a neurotransmitter that produces euphoric sensations in the brain. Once a man has ejaculated, the levels of dopamine drop significantly. In addition, there are increased levels of oxytocin and serotonin, the latter of which has a calming effect on the man's brain. While oxytocin promotes social contact, the high levels of testosterone in a man's brain at this time suppress the chemical and allow serotonin to take over, making him feel sleepy.

While the same chemical changes occur in a woman's brain during and after sex, the oestrogen in her brain is far more responsive to oxytocin, which then has a stronger effect than the serotonin. Women also have a naturally higher level of oxytocin in their brains. These factors help to prevent a woman from becoming tired and make her more inclined to talk and cuddle after sex.

To compound the chemical results of male ejaculation, sex frequently takes place at night, when a man is already inherently tired. This can be caused by the late hour or a large meal or alcohol consumed shortly before sex.

WHY IS 'GOD BLESS YOU' SAID AFTER A SNEEZE?

The expression 'God bless you', or sometimes just 'bless you', is commonly said to people after they sneeze. As with many sayings, its exact origin is unclear.

It's thought that the saying originally served as a literal blessing. On his accession to the papacy in AD 590, at the outbreak of the bubonic plague, Pope Gregory the Great ordered his priests and subjects to look towards God for help and guidance during the troubled times. Sneezing was thought to be a sign that someone might be about to contract the plague, so the Catholic Church exhorted its followers to say 'God bless you' to ward off the disease.

Another common theory of the origin of the phrase is the early belief that the act of sneezing would expel the person's soul from his or her body. 'God bless you' was thus said to protect the unguarded soul from the Devil until the person's body regained it. Similarly, in the Middle Ages it was thought by some that a sneeze was the expulsion of an evil spirit from the body, and so after a sneeze the person was blessed in the hope that the evil spirit would be prevented from returning.

A further explanation lies in the ancient belief that the heart stopped briefly when a person sneezed, and so the blessing was made in an attempt to restore life to the person.

It's likely that one of the origins listed above brought about the custom, which has continued through the ages and is now present in many languages and cultures.

WHY CAN'T YOU TICKLE YOURSELF?
This is a question that has bedevilled philosophers as far back as Aristotle.

Scientists believe that, when we are tickled, our bodies panic and enter a defensive state. This reaction is thought to have developed in our early ancestors in response to the attack of certain types of predator, such as spiders, whose progress across the skin the act of tickling is said to mimic. In modern times, because we know there is no danger, our reaction to being tickled is to laugh, either because we're not prepared to be tickled and it takes us by surprise or because of the anticipation of being tickled and not knowing exactly when or where it will occur.

The area of the brain that deals with co-ordination and sensory signals when we move is the cerebellum. It is here that our brain determines what to expect when the body performs movements and where it differentiates between expected and unexpected sensations, ignoring expected sensations caused by the body's own movements and yet being very sensitive to unexpected ones. One example of this in action is that people don't notice their tongue movements when they talk or eat. Similarly, when we try to tickle ourselves, we are in control of the movement; the element of surprise is lost and our brain predicts where we're going to touch ourselves and prepares for this. There is no natural internal tension or panic and no corresponding reaction like that which occurs when others tickle us. These 'self-awareness signals' are delivered by the brain in a split second – too fast for us to fool ourselves and preventing us, therefore, from tickling ourselves.

Charles Darwin believed that tickling was a form of social interaction, making people laugh through the anticipation of pleasure. He postulated that for tickling to be effective the recipient must not be aware of the exact point of contact, which is why people are unable to tickle themselves.

It is thought that some schizophrenics, who at times suffer from delusions and have difficulty distinguishing self-generated from external touch, may be able to tickle themselves because they are unaware of the precise point of contact.

WHY DOES HUMAN HAIR TURN GREY?

The bane of many people's existence, greying hair, is due to a phenomenon known as *poliosis*, derived from the Greek word *polios*, meaning 'grey'. Why some people's hair turns grey and others does not is still not entirely clear.

The root of every hair is covered with tubing known as a *follicle*. Each follicle contains a number of pigment cells that hold a substance called *melanin*, which is distributed through the hair shaft, giving the hair its particular colour. As people age, their hair often turns from its normal colour to grey because there is a gradual decrease of melanin in the pigment cells. When this ceases to be produced in the root of the hair, the hair grows without any pigmentation and is grey or white.

Different people turn grey at different times because of their genetics. Men often start at around the age of thirty while women tend to start a little later, at around thirty-five. While there's no medical evidence to suggest that any nutrients, vitamins or other substances can prevent hair from turning grey, some studies have alluded to the fact that a smoker's hair is more likely to turn grey than a non-smoker's. In addition, a lack of nutrients and some treatments for AIDS and cancer are thought to be the cause of premature greying. However, scientists do not believe that being shocked or stressed increases the likelihood of going grey.

The age at which a person's hair turns grey is not thought to be related to the hair's original colour, although greying hair is often more noticeable on dark-haired people because of the contrast in colour. There is also thought to be no link between the greying of the hair and balding.

WHY DO MANY PRICES END IN NINETY-NINE PENCE?

In the UK, a widely used practice among retailers is

to market goods so that the prices end in ninety-nine pence. A similar practice occurs in many parts of the world, such as the US, where many goods are priced at so many dollars and ninety-nine cents. This is a phenomenon sometimes known as 'the nine fixation' and is thought to have begun in the late nineteenth century.

Goods are priced this way for a number of reasons, the predominant one of which is that people instinctively round the price down to the leading digit, so a price of £10.99 will be viewed as £10, which might persuade people to purchase as they subconsciously think they're getting a bargain. It also gives the impression that the retailer has discounted the price from the next rounded number. Psychologists claim that another reason for people to be seduced by this kind of marketing is that they view the shopping experience more favourably if they receive change. By ending a price with ninety-nine pence, the retailer therefore gives the person the smallest amount of change possible, again maximising profits.

Another possible reason for this kind of marketing is that people find the look of a combination of nines appealing. The aesthetic value of something priced at £99.99, for example, might therefore make a person more inclined to purchase it.

It is also thought that the practice of such

pricing actually started as a means of ensuring that cashiers had to open the cash register to give change, which made it more difficult for them simply to steal the money that had been given to them. Another, more compelling explanation is that it allows the use of gimmicks such as advertising goods as being 'under £100'. By making the item £99.99, the retailer is true to his word and might succeed in luring the customer into the store where other items might then be purchased. Some claim, however, that this method does not work because nine is a larger number than one and £99.99 has more digits than £100, and so seems more expensive. It can also prove counter-productive by causing confusion and annoyance among consumers, who might feel that they are being duped.

WHAT IS THE DIFFERENCE BETWEEN AIDS AND HIV?

HIV (Human Immunodeficiency Virus) is the virus that causes the disease called AIDS (Acquired Immune Deficiency [or Immunodeficiency] Syndrome). Being HIV positive means that a person has HIV but not necessarily AIDS. This person might not exhibit any symptoms of the infection, depending on how much damage the virus has done, but a person with

AIDS will be HIV positive and will display symptoms of the illness.

HIV attacks and damages the human immune system, killing off healthy immune-system cells. AIDS, meanwhile, is the disease that results from being infected with HIV. It is a progressive disease that destroys the body's immunity, making it unable to fight germs and infections adequately. The virus generally enters the body through contact with bodily fluid, such as blood or semen, eventually taking hold until the person cannot stave off infections, making them more susceptible to illness and disease. It is this final advanced stage of the viral infection that is known as AIDS.

HIV is thought to have originated from African monkeys carrying a closely related simian virus and is believed to have passed to humans in the early twentieth century through their interaction with humans (for example, blood transference while being hunted by humans). It is then likely to have spread throughout Africa and then the Western world, mainly by sexual activity. During the 1980s, AIDS was noticed to be largely present among drug users and homosexuals.

At present, millions of people worldwide have AIDS. It is currently incurable, although with treatment people have lived for many years after acquiring the disease.

HOW CAN DIRECTION BE FOUND WITHOUT A COMPASS?

Direction can be found during both day and night, in both hemispheres, without the need for a compass. The simplest ways of finding direction are to use a wristwatch or to observe the moon and stars.

During the day, a normal analogue wristwatch is the most useful commonplace tool. It must be set to the normal local time of where you are and held horizontal to the ground. If you're in the northern hemisphere, point the hour hand at the sun and bisect the angle between the hour hand and twelve o'clock. This bisected line points north–south, with south pointing away from you and the watch. In the southern hemisphere, point twelve o'clock at the sun and bisect the angle between it and the hour hand to give the same north–south line, with north pointing away from you and the watch. The further you are from the equator, the more accurate this method becomes. If you don't have an analogue watch, using the above methods with a pencil drawing of a watch showing the correct time will also work.

At nighttime, direction can be determined by observing the moon and stars. If the moon rises before the sun sets, its western side will be illuminated, while this will be the eastern side if it rises after the sun sets. In the northern hemisphere, the star constellation Ursa Major, known as the Plough (or Big Dipper), and Cassiopeia (which looks like a W) can also be used to determine direction. These constellations never set and circle the Pole Star (Polaris) on opposite sides to each other. To determine direction, draw a line between them to find the Pole Star, then draw another line perpendicular from the Pole Star to Earth. The point at which the line intersects with the horizon is north.

In the southern hemisphere, the constellation to look for is the Southern Cross (Crus), a prominent, crucifix-shaped grouping as depicted on the Australian flag. To determine direction, draw a line below the cross that's four and a half times the length of the cross but along the same line as the length of the cross. From this point, drop perpendicular to the ground. The intersection point on the horizon indicates due south.

WHY DO PEOPLE HAVE AN APPENDIX?

The vermiform appendix – or, simply, the appendix – is a wormlike tube that has only one end and is connected to the caecum in the right lower abdomen of humans. Its name is from the Latin word meaning 'wormlike'.

The appendix is prone to becoming infected, an

ailment known as *appendicitis* that causes it to become inflamed and painful, at which point it must be removed – via an operation known as an *appendectomy* – because it bursts and floods the bloodstream with toxins, which can prove fatal. Appendicitis is less common in people whose diet is high in fibre, consisting of a lot of fruit and vegetables. Given that the appendix is so often removed without any later consequences to the person, people often question why we have one in the first place.

The purpose and function of the appendix are not fully understood and remain subjects of debate. Some believe the appendix plays a role in our immune systems and is a useful organ of the lymphatic system, others think it has a function that has not yet been discovered and still others think that it's needed for only a short time after we are born. However, the traditional and still prevailing view is that it was an organ that played a practical role in the digestive systems of our vegetarian ancestors. It has not disappeared through evolution and has remained with us as a vestigial organ, having no function today. This theory is supported by the fact that some modern animals have a similar organ that functions to process fibre, just as the appendix might have done for our ancestors.

WHY DO GOLF BALLS HAVE DIMPLES?

Dimples have been a feature of golf balls for over 100 years. Most balls have between 350 and 400 dimples on them, which are situated to make the ball as symmetrical as possible. They were first introduced when golfers found that roughed-up and dented balls travelled much further than smooth balls. In fact, dimpled balls generally travel up to four times further than smooth balls owing to the laws of aerodynamics.

The two major forces that impact on a ball as it travels through the air are lift and drag. Lift works on the ball in a perpendicular manner, while drag impedes the forward motion of the ball, and the varying levels of these forces affect the layer of air surrounding the ball while it is in flight. The dimples act to change this layer of air by increasing the lift and reducing the drag. Smooth balls, of course, do not do this. A smooth ball drags a large wake of air behind it, which slows the ball, while a dimpled ball grabs the air stream, keeping it very close by and increases the turbulence of the air, redirecting the higher-pressured air behind the ball and stopping it from separating as quickly as it would normally. This pocket of air stays attached to the ball for longer, reducing the wake and forcing the ball to travel further.

Most balls are hit with backspin, which gives them lift by causing the top layer of air on the ball to travel faster than the lower layer. This velocity reduces pressure, so the pressure on top of the ball is less that that exerted from below, and this difference in pressure creates an upward lift on the ball. By forcing the air to stay attached to the ball, dimples help to increase this difference in pressure, thus increasing the lift and enabling the ball to travel a longer distance.

The number of dimples on a golf ball must be balanced against their size. Too many small dimples, for instance, make a ball seem smooth, rendering their aerodynamic contouring ineffective. The 350–400 dimples currently found on modern balls has been found to be the optimum number.

WHAT IS THE ORIGIN OF THE TERM 'OK'?

As tends to be the case with the origins of sayings, the starting point of OK (pronounced 'okay') is a matter of contention. Indeed, the etymological sources of few other expressions have quite so many opposing views. Some of the term's supposed origins are as follows:

- a railroad freight agent, Obadiah Kelly, who initialled bills of lading;
- the wood out of which British ships were built –

oak – which is a durable wood and gave rise to the saying that such wood was 'oak-a';

- the German words *ohne Korrektur*, meaning 'no changes', in relation to publishing houses marking manuscripts with the initials;
- the ancient Greek schooling practice of marking the letters on exceptional papers, indicating that they were *ola kala* (literally 'it is good');
- a telegraphic signal that meant 'open key';
- an army biscuits supplier, O. Kendall & Sons, whose initials were stamped on each tin of biscuits;
- a German general who signed documents OK to indicate his rank ('Ober-Kommando');
- the French words 'aux Cayes' (Cayes being a port that produced high-quality rum);
- US military records stating that there were no casualties – that is, zero killed ('0K');
- the Finnish word *oikea*, meaning 'correct';
- the African words meaning 'all right', introduced to the US during the time of slavery;
- the Scottish phrase *och aye*;
- a worker at Ford Motor Company called either Otto Kruger or Oskar Krause supposedly writing his initials on inspected cars;
- the Choctaw Indian word *okeh*, used by US president Andrew Jackson in an 1815 battle.

The most favoured derivation, however, probably because it is supported by documentary evidence, is that it stems from a phrase used in the nineteenth century. It was a fad during the 1830s in Boston for newspapers to use comical expressions such as KY for 'know yuse', OW for 'oll wright', NS for 'nuff said' and, notably, OK for 'oll korrect'. This habit soon spread to New York and New Orleans. OK became popular in 1840 when the supporters of the Democratic politician Martin Van Buren formed the OK Club. In this case, the letters stood for 'Old Kinderhook' (Kinderhook, New York, being Van Buren's place of birth), and it's thought that it was through this use of the letters that they were brought into mainstream usage under their current definition.

Lending weight to this theory, it's said that a 1935 US court case decided that the initials 'OK' written on the invoices of a Japanese rice merchant stood for 'oll korrect'.

DOES AN ELEPHANT TRULY NEVER FORGET?

It's a common expression that elephants never forget. In fact, one of the collective nouns for a group of elephants is a 'memory'. The common conception of elephants having great memories has been put to the test over the years by scientists and researchers and found to be true: elephants *do* have exceptional long-term memories.

An experiment conducted in the 1950s that tested an elephant's recall by showing it various wooden boxes showed that the animal had a remarkable ability to retain information. Many later experiments have produced similar results; in some instances, the testers believe that the elephant uses no particular strategy for recall as some animals do, but instead merely remembers effortlessly. These tests have been backed up by circus-elephant trainers, who have attested to the amazing recall of their animals, asserting that they can learn up to 100 different commands and remember them for years. Elephants have also been found never to forget someone who has either cared for or mistreated them.

The elephant's incredible memory is particularly acute among the female matriarchs, who lead the herd (the males leave at an early age) and are able to recognise any outsider elephant as friend or foe based on their prior experience of that elephant. Such discrimination enables the rest of the herd to prosper, as they are able to feed and relax without needing to be on the lookout for danger. The matriarch is also able to lead the herd over long distances to places rich with food and water and, in dry times, she is able to find water sources that she has not visited in many years.

Combined with elephants' excellent memory is their high level of general intelligence, as demonstrated in the attention they lavish on to their newborn offspring and the way in which they grieve over the losses of loved ones. Indeed, elephants have been known to stand vigil over a dead friend and even stop to pay their respects at times when they later pass the place at which the death took place. Elephant herds also have an intricate social structure, which is indicative of intelligent animals.

WHY DOES SWEAT SMELL?

When people are exposed to heat, through experiencing elevated air temperature, exercise or emotional stress, they often sweat. The perspiration produced is a healthy and natural part of the body's thermostatic mechanism; when it evaporates from the skin, this process cools the body. However, the degree to which people sweat and the resulting smell that is produced varies greatly.

The skin has two types of sweat glands: eccrine and apocrine. The skin contains millions of eccrine glands, distributed all over the body, and the fluid that they produce consists mainly of salt and water and has no smell. Apocrine glands, meanwhile, tend to be located in areas where there are a lot of hair follicles, such as under the arms, around the genitals and on the head, and the sweat that they produce is fatty. While the sweat from apocrine glands also has no smell, it is a source of nutrition for bacteria on the skin, which break it down, releasing natural chemicals and excrement that produce the unpleasant smell of body odour. This process is particularly noticeable on the feet. Each foot generally contains 250,000 sweat glands and tends to sweat more than other parts of the body. Compounding this are the socks and shoes that provide the feeding bacteria with ideal warm and damp conditions, which also trap the sweat and the resultant odour from the feeding bacteria.

Levels and intensity of body odour vary between different people because some have larger and more active apocrine glands and more aggressive skin bacteria than others. In addition, the nature of the sweat generated by the apocrine glands can be influenced by mood, the consumption of certain foods and drink (such as spicy food, alcohol and caffeine), the use of drugs, hormone levels, and medical and hereditary conditions.

Body odour from sweat can be reduced by washing regularly with soap, wearing clean clothes and using a deodorant (which kills bacteria) or antiperspirant (which blocks the pores of the skin, preventing the release of sweat).

WHY DOES METAL RUST?

Rusting is a very destructive form of oxidisation (ie reaction to oxygen) that occurs in iron and metals containing iron. Rust forms as an orange substance on the iron, weakening it by replacing it with flaky powder until eventually the metal disintegrates. Other metals oxidise to form compounds similar to rust, and in these cases the process is commonly known as *corrosion* rather than *rusting*. Rust is a specific type of corrosion that occurs only when iron is present.

Rust is the common name for the compound called iron oxide, which is a combination of iron and oxygen. Oxygen that is in the air does not react with iron because it is combined with other oxygen particles, but when water comes into contact with iron it combines with carbon dioxide in the air to form an acid that dissolves the iron and allows the water to break into its hydrogen and oxygen parts. The free oxygen is then able to combine with the iron to form iron oxide – rust. This process frees electrons, allowing them to flow to another piece of metal or to a different point on the iron, where further rusting occurs.

Iron rusts more quickly when exposed to seawater

and salt spray than when it is in contact with pure water. This is because of the presence of sodium-chloride ions, which making this type of water more conductive and which in turn speeds up the corroding processes. Rust is also permeable to air and water, which allows rusting to continue deeper into the metal.

Covering metals with protective paints can help to prevent rusting from taking place, but rust can still form anywhere that the paint is scratched. Galvanising metals by covering them with a protective layer of zinc is another way of preventing or inhibiting the rusting process, as the iron beneath it is still protected even if the galvanising is scratched, as the zinc is more susceptible to corrosive elements and will be broken down instead. Such protection is used to prevent rusting on ships and underground pipes. Magnesium is similar to zinc in its susceptibility to corrosion and is often used in the same way, placed at points on iron-based materials, where it rusts instead of the iron underneath.

WHY DO WE HAVE EAR WAX?

What we call 'ear wax' is not actually wax but a sticky yellow substance called cerumen, which is secreted by glands in the outer ear canals of humans and some animals. Cerumen plays a number of essential roles for the ear, such as keeping the ear canal lubricated, which prevents irritation and itching of the skin, and providing protection against some strains of bacteria and fungi in the ear canal.

Probably the most vital role played by ear wax, however, is its cleaning function. With the help of movements of the jaw, cerumen makes its way to the opening of the ear, where it can be washed away, taking with it any dirt, dust and other foreign material that might have lodged in the canal, thus preventing blockages and ear infections. In addition to this active cleaning process, ear wax coats the outer ear canal, trapping dirt and germs and preventing them from reaching the sensitive ear drum.

There is, however, a further function that scientists believe ear wax fulfils: it's thought that the bitter taste of ear wax acts as a repellent to insects. In the event that it doesn't repel insects, its sticky texture acts to trap and immobilise them, stopping them from entering further into the canal. They can then be removed via the ear's self-cleaning process.

WHY DO PEOPLE SHRINK WITH AGE?

Both men and women shrink in height after the age of thirty. Generally speaking, a man might shrink 3cm in his lifetime and a woman 5cm. This is all part of the natural aging process, whereby people progressively lose muscle and fat from their bodies. When this happens, gravity forces the vertebrae in the spine to degenerate, compress and eventually collapse into each other, resulting in a loss of height.

The shrinking process is exacerbated by a condition called osteoporosis, a condition that predominantly affects older people, where the spongy tissue inside their bones is broken down and not replaced, resulting in a dramatic reduction in bone density. This process can also result in the vertebrae becoming crushed together, which is often why some old people are stooped and cannot stand up straight. A lack of calcium in older people might also result in less bone density and a consequent shrinkage in height.

The shrinking process can be reduced by eating a well-balanced diet rich in calcium, which strengthens the bones. Regular exercise also slows the process, helping to keep the bones and muscles strong.

People don't only shrink as they get older, however; they also shrink during the course of one day, by a height of several millimetres. This is due to the water contained in the discs of the spine being compressed by gravity, which in effect makes a person shorter. By the next morning, however, the body recovers and returns to its normal height.

WHERE DID THE FABRIC DENIM ORIGINATE AND WHY IS IT STITCHED WITH ORANGE THREAD?

It's common knowledge that the word *denim* is derived from the French phrase 'serge de Nimes', which means 'serge from Nimes', relating to a town in southern France where the fabric was first made, and that the phrase eventually became corrupted and contracted to simply 'denim'.

Then, in the 1850s, a Bavarian named Levi Strauss set up a wholesale clothing business in San Francisco. In 1872, Levi received a letter from a Russian immigrant from Nevada named Jacob Davis, who had come up with the idea of adding metal rivets to the fabric to increase its durability. The following year, Jacob and Levi began to work together, employing this method of manufacture, using orange stitching that matched the similarly coloured copper rivets.

Like *denim*, the word *jeans* also derives from a town – Genoa, in Italy – and is short for the phrase 'Jean fustian', where 'Jean' is actually a modern spelling of Jannes, the French word for Genoa, and 'fustian' means cotton cloth. Before 1873, Levi Strauss bought 'jeans pants' (a term used for clothing made from jean fustian) from the eastern US to sell in the west of the country. When denim later became a more popular fabric for workwear because of its durability, the term 'jeans' was still used as a term for the denim trousers.

Denim jeans have now become so popular and widespread that they are a part of modern culture.

WHY DO MEN HAVE NIPPLES?

Once a human embryo has been conceived, no matter what its ultimate gender, it follows a female template, adopting all female characteristics, including nipples. After a number of weeks in this state, a certain gene in the male embryo stimulates the production of the male hormone testosterone, which prompts the embryo to develop masculine qualities. While the nipples remain present (because they are formed before this process takes place), they will not function in the way that they would have had the embryo been supplied with female hormones.

Not only do male babies have nipples, but they are also born with breast tissue and milk ducts and glands. These are normally inoperative, but, if men experience increased levels of the female hormone oestrogen and a lack of testosterone, they can develop breasts like those of women and, in extreme cases, even perform lactation. Because men have breast tissue, they are at risk from breast cancer, albeit to a far lesser extent than women are.

It is thought by some that men might once have used nipples to help feed their young during lean times. Now that this no longer occurs, it has been asked of scientists why evolution has not done away with these superfluous male nipples. The common response is that, because diseases affecting the nipples are rare in men, there is no genetic imperative to do away with the nipples, and so they simply remain.

WHAT IS COCA-COLA MADE FROM AND DID IT ONCE CONTAIN COCAINE?

Since its invention, the ingredients of Coca-Cola have been kept a long-guarded secret, which has both prevented others from copying the exact formula and, over the years, enhanced the public's perception of what a unique product Coca-Cola is.

Coca-Cola was named in 1886 because of its two main ingredients: kola nuts and extract of coca leaves – ie cocaine, which the drink did contain until 1929, although in very small amounts.

The exact balance of the recipe, however, has never been disclosed to the public, and the original copy of it is locked in the vault of the Sun Trust Bank in Atlanta, USA. It has commonly been said that only two executives originally knew the formula, and that each of them knew only half of it. In fact, the Coca-Cola Company does have a rule that only two executives can know the formula, but each knows the entire formula. When air travel became popular, it became company policy not to allow both of the executives to fly on the same plane.

While the exact recipe of Coke remains a mystery, it is generally accepted that it comprises the following key flavourings: cinnamon, nutmeg, lime, lemon, orange, coriander, caramel, coco, neroli and vanilla.

WHAT IS THE PURPOSE OF PUBIC HAIR AND WHY IS IT CURLY?

The purpose of pubic hair is something that has been argued about for years. Even today, scientists are still unsure of its function.

One view is that pubic hair protects against friction during sexual intercourse, as well as providing cushioning for the pelvis in that area. Another view is that it provided insulation for our ancestors, although this is not widely held because of the lack of significant hair over the rest of our bodies. However, there is some support for the idea that the hair helps to regulate body temperature in the genital area, which is particularly important for the production of sperm in men.

Pubic hair also performs two other possible functions. The first is that it indicates that the person is sexually mature and able to procreate; indeed, some anthropologists have suggested that pubic hair in males might have been an ancient way of impressing and deterring other males who were in competition with them, performing the same function as a mane on a lion. The second proposed function is that it helps to trap and retain the pheromones that are secreted from sweat glands in the pubic area, which are thought to serve as a powerful aphrodisiac to the opposite gender.

Pubic hair is curly because for some reason our sex hormones turn the hair follicles in that area into an oval shape, which in turn makes the hair oval in shape, causing it to bend. Straight hair grows from round follicles and is less prone to curliness.

WHAT IS ACID RAIN AND WHAT CAUSES IT?

Acid rain is one of the most dangerous and widespread forms of air pollution and is caused by the smoke and gases that are expelled by cars and factories that use fossil fuels. These fuels contain sulphur and when they are burned the sulphur reacts with oxygen in the air to form sulphur dioxide. The high-temperature burning of these fuels in industry also releases nitrogen monoxide and dioxide. Once these oxides are airborne, they react with water to form sulphuric and nitric acid. These acids are soluble and so, when it rains, they fall with the rain. Such precipitation is literally a mixture of acid and rain. To be classed as acid rain, it must have a pH of below 4.0. (The pH of normal rain is about 5.6.)

While volcanoes and natural biological processes in oceans and wetlands contribute to the levels of airborne sulphur dioxide and nitrogen oxides, and therefore acid rain, the increase has been caused predominately by the burning of fossil fuels since the Industrial Revolution. Indeed, it was first reported in Manchester in 1852.

Acid rain is a widespread problem because the gases can be transported for long distances before they are converted to acid and fall as rain. In addition, its corrosive nature has serious implications, causing widespread damage to the environment, depleting fish stocks and harming trees and other plant life. This can affect other animals dependent on fish and plants and can damage entire ecosystems. It can also affect humans directly, polluting water supplies, as well as corroding buildings, cars and anything made of metal or stone.

WHY DID KENTUCKY FRIED CHICKEN CHANGE ITS NAME TO KFC?

When in 1991 the fast-food chain Kentucky Fried Chicken changed its name to KFC, it was suggested at the time that this move was in response to a study carried out by the University of New Hampshire that proved that real chickens weren't being used in the food. Instead, so the story goes, genetically modified animals with no beaks or feathers were being used in order to save on costs. Because of this, it was said, government regulations dictated that such mutated animals could not be marketed as chickens and so the company was force to omit the word 'chicken' from its name, as well as from advertisements and menus. This, of course, is a myth. No such study was undertaken and the claim has no basis in fact.

There were a number of genuine reasons behind the name change. One was to lessen the emphasis on the word 'chicken', because the company was at that point providing a more diverse menu, while another was to remove the word 'fried', which had unhealthy connotations for increasingly health-conscious consumers. A third reason was the growing trend of major companies to shorten their names and to use only initials. As most people referred to the company as KFC anyway, it seemed only logical to embrace the name.

IS DRINKING TOO MUCH WATER BAD FOR YOU?

It *is* possible to drink too much water. When this happens, the result is water intoxication, a condition known in medical terms as *hyponatremia*.

Hyponatremia occurs when the body's sodium

levels fall dangerously low, which can happen when an excessive amount of water has been ingested, causing a dramatic boost in the levels of blood plasma. This dilutes the salt content of the blood, which is further reduced by sweating, and thus reduces the amount of salt available to the tissues in the body, which can lead to swelling in the brain and a leaking of fluid into the lungs. It also affects muscle and heart function. The symptoms of hyponatremia are usually headaches, dizziness, nausea and fatigue. It can cause seizures, unconsciousness and even death.

Hyponatremia occurs rarely, however, and, when it does, it's usually suffered by athletes who have exerted themselves for a long period of time, losing a lot of salt through sweating then rehydrating with plain water. There have been a number of cases in the last ten years of people dying from this condition while running long distances.

Hyponatremia can be prevented by eating salty foods and drinking sports drinks specially designed to replace lost electrolytes. It is recommended by some that people should drink only when they are thirsty, and that athletes should drink only as much as they sweat. An oft-quoted suggested amount to drink is six to eight cups of water per day.

WHY ARE UNIDENTIFIED PEOPLE CALLED JOHN AND JANE DOE?

John Doe is traditionally the name used for an unknown party in legal actions. In such cases, if a second name was needed, Richard Roe was used (doe being a female deer and roe being a species of European deer). If third and fourth names were needed, John Stiles and Richard Miles were used. The female equivalent of John Doe was Jane Doe, while the name Mary Major was also sometimes used.

The use of John Doe as a substitute name is thought to date back to King Edward III's reign in fourteenth-century England, where the name was apparently used to identify a hypothetical landowner in a legal action for the ejection of a tenant, who was named Richard Roe. This precedent and the names involved became famous and were referred to in various legal commentaries in the eighteenth century. It's not known why these particular names were selected, but it's likely that they were common Christian names at the time and so symbolically represented the general public. It's also likely that they didn't derive from real people bearing those names.

The use of the names John and Jane Doe as substitutes for unknown or undisclosed identities has survived to this day.

DOES CHEWING GUM REALLY TAKE SEVEN YEARS TO DIGEST?

While many agree that the body does not digest chewing gum, it doesn't take seven years to pass through the human digestive system. This claim might have resulted from the word 'indigestible' being commonly associated with chewing gum, and might also have arisen from parents' warnings to their children not to swallow gum, or from the fact that gum remains largely the same size and consistency after hours of chewing.

It's true that chewing gum does resist the body's attempts to break it down, but it takes the same amount of time to pass through the digestive system as most foods. A large percentage of the gum is not digested by the body and so passes through relatively unchanged. The same thing happens with foods containing cellulose, or fibre.

While there is a very low risk of chewing gum remaining lodged in the body, it is generally advisable not to swallow it.

HOW DO CROCODILES AND ALLIGATORS DIFFER?

Crocodiles are reptiles that comprise fourteen species of the *Crocodylidae* family across Australia, Africa and the Americas. The two largest species, the saltwater and the Nile crocodiles, are dangerous predators that kill hundreds of people every year. All crocodiles live in salt water and have powerful jaws and teeth, and they can grow to lengths of up to 23ft.

Alligators, meanwhile, are closely related to crocodiles and comprise two species of the *Alligatoridae* family, one in North America and one in China (they are closely related to the caiman that appears in Central and South America). These reptiles grow up to 12ft long and have a shorter and broader snout than the crocodile. An alligator's teeth are concealed when its mouth is shut, whereas a crocodile's are visible.

Alligators also tend to be greyish-black in colour, compared with the lightly tanned crocodiles. They are also far more timid than crocodiles and have slightly different foot webbing. Unlike the crocodile's salt glands, which excrete excess salt, the alligator's don't function. The crocodile also has sensory pits all over its body, while the alligator only has them near its jaws.

In essence, there aren't too many differences between crocodiles and alligators. The main differences between the two are that the crocodile is far larger and more aggressive.

Some confusion results from Australian saltwater crocodiles sometimes being incorrectly referred to as alligators. Indeed, there are a number of rivers in northern Australia with the word 'Alligator' in their names, but these were actually misnamed after the crocodiles that inhabit them.

CAN IT BE TOO COLD TO SNOW?

On very cold days, people sometimes remark that it is too cold to snow, but is this possible? In fact, snow can fall at any temperature; indeed, snow sometimes falls in Antarctica, where the temperatures are extremely low. However, snow rarely falls when the air is very cold, as this usually indicates high pressure and dry air, conditions that aren't conducive to snow formation.

Snow forms when moist air rises and attaches to dust. If the temperature is low enough, the water condenses and freezes to form snowflakes, while, if the air is too dry, there isn't enough water to form the snow. The heaviest falls of snow usually occur when the ambient temperature is around 0°C. Any warmer and it rains instead.

WHY DO WE HICCUP, AND WHAT CAUSES THEM?

If the diaphragm becomes irritated, it can spasm involuntarily, which can cause you to gulp air. This sudden inrush of air to the lungs makes the glottis (the opening at the top of the air passage) close, producing the classic 'hic' sound.

The diaphragm can become irritated by a number of factors, such as spicy food, too much food or food passing too quickly, excessive drinking, coughing or laughing. It can also react to nervousness and excitement.

Hiccups generally pass in a few minutes, although they can last for days, in which case they are usually indicative of some other sort of medical problem. They currently perform no known function, and it's not known whether they had a purpose in our ancestors, either. Some scientists believe that they were originally necessary to ventilate the gills in water-breathing animals and that the action has persisted all the way through to humans, while others think that they help babies to suckle, the closing of the glottis preventing milk from entering the lungs.

There are many home remedies for hiccups, most of which tend to be based on disrupting the hiccup cycle. They include breathing into a paper bag, drinking water from the opposite side of the cup, eating a spoonful of sugar or honey, being startled or concentrating hard on the hiccupping. In most cases, hiccups are harmless and pass of their own accord after a few minutes.

WHY DID THE ROMANS WEAR TOGAS?

In the days of the Roman Empire, most Roman men wore garments that consisted of a tunic of knee-length material, fastened with a belt. Over the tunic was then worn a toga, which consisted of a long sash of cloth draped over the left shoulder and folded in a specific manner. While tunics were worn as everyday clothes, togas were classed as being formal attire, similar to the modern-day suit, and were worn on special occasions.

Togas were a sign of citizenship in Rome; outsiders weren't permitted to wear them. Originally worn at all times, later in the Roman Empire they were generally worn only at official functions as a mark of status. They also came in different colours to indicate the rank and position of their wearer, plain togas being worn by the lower classes and brightly coloured, ornate togas symbolising power, wealth and status.

It is thought that the term 'purple patch', referring to a period of wealth and prosperity, is derived from the attire of Roman noblemen, who wore purple togas and were provided with everything they wanted.

WHY DO ONIONS MAKE PEOPLE CRY?

It's not the strong odour of onions that makes us cry when we cut them but the gas that they emit, which is also responsible for their pungent taste and for the bad breath they can cause.

Onions contain a sulphur-based oil. When cut, the cells that contain the sulphur compounds are broken and the compounds are converted into sulfenic acid, which in turn produces a highly volatile chemical called syn-propanethial-S-oxide, which then rises into the air. When this chemical comes into contact with our eyes, it reacts with the moisture in our eyelids and results in the production of sulphuric acid, which irritates the eyes and stimulates the lachrymal glands. When stimulated, these glands release tears to flush out the acid and protect the eye. Rubbing the eyes with the hands can often exacerbate the problem, especially if the hands are covered with oil from the onion.

There are a variety of ways of preventing the gases emitted by the onion from reaching the eyes. Moving your head away from the onion so that the gas disperses is one such method, while another is to cook the onion first, or even cool it in the fridge, which both serve to change the compounds in the onion. Breathing with an open mouth can also help, as it means you'll suck away some of the gases before they reach your eyes. Probably the best and easiest method, however, is to cut the onion under running water, which washes away the gases before they can reach the eyes.

WHY IS GETTING MARRIED CALLED 'TYING THE KNOT'?

There are a variety of possible sources for the origin of this saying. One suggests that brides in the eighteenth century wore knots of coloured ribbons attached to their wedding gown, while another states that the term derives from the Celtic hand-fasting ritual in which the man and wife's hands were bound and tied to signify their union and the completion of the wedding ceremony. A more common explanation, however, stems from the fact that at one time beds were made from planks of wood held together by rope. On the wedding night, the bed was thought to require additional strength and stability from an extra knotted rope as the couple consummated their vows.

Similar to this is the phrase 'to sleep tight', the origin of which is thought to derive from the frames of such beds being sprung with ropes. If the ropes went slack, it resulted in an uncomfortable night's sleep. The ropes had to be tight so that a person could 'sleep tight' (ie well).

DO SWIMMING POOLS REALLY CONTAIN A CHEMICAL THAT REVEALS URINE?

Parents and swimming-pool attendants are often heard adamantly stating that a chemical is added to the water to reveal the presence of urine. It's said that, if someone urinates in a public pool, the chemical will react with the urine and produce a trail of purple or red dye, leading to the culprit. Suppliers of pool products have been inundated over the years with requests for this magical substance. Unfortunately, no such chemical exists, nor has it ever existed. The mythical dye is an imaginary invention whose existence is perpetuated by parents in an attempt to prevent their children from committing the indiscretion. Experts suggest that, if such a chemical could be made, it would be difficult to stop it from reacting with other organisms present in the water.

In reality, the amount of urine in a swimming pool is such a small percentage, compared with the volume of water, that it is negligible and insignificant, constituting only a chemical trace.

HOW DOES THE ATKINS DIET WORK?

The Atkins diet has received a lot of publicity over recent years, with many celebrities experimenting with it, but there has also been much debate over its effectiveness and its implications on health and wellbeing.

The diet was invented by Dr Robert Atkins, whose books claim that weight gain is caused by ingesting carbohydrates, a major energy source contained in foods such as pasta, rice and potatoes. The diet also suggests its adherents reduce their sugar intake and, instead, eat fat and protein. It also recommends nutritional supplements and exercise.

This change of diet alters the body's metabolism so that it burns fat instead of the glucose contained in carbohydrates. Where virtually no carbohydrates are present, the body is forced to use fat as its energy source instead in a process known as *lipolysis*, which begins when the body enters a state of *ketosis* (ie a fasting mode) because it has no carbohydrates to burn. A lack of carbohydrates also results in the body releasing less insulin, a hormone that controls the levels of sugar in the blood and causes sugar that isn't burned by the body's cells to be stored as fat. When less sugar and carbohydrates are eaten, less insulin is secreted and the body burns fat for fuel, resulting in a loss in weight.

Critics of the diet claim that high levels of protein from foods such as meat are associated with heart conditions, cancer, osteoporosis and kidney damage. They also claim that people often put weight back on once they stop following the diet and that, by not being provided with certain food groups, the body is lacking the nutrients it needs in order to stay healthy. Additionally, critics claim that the diet is unhealthy for people who exercise, for whom carbohydrates are an essential energy source.

WHAT MAKES STOMACHS GROWL?

The growling or rumbling noises that the stomach makes is actually caused by muscular activity in the walls of the stomach and small intestines. The medical term for it is *borborygmi*, a Greek term that translates as 'rumbling'.

The sound is produced as a result of contractions of the stomach, which serve to break down ingested food and move gas and fluids to prevent them from accumulating in one place. These movements produce vibrations, and it is these vibrations that cause the rumbling sounds.

A growling stomach is often associated with hunger, but, in fact, the noise can be produced by a full or empty stomach, although it's often heard more clearly when the stomach is empty because there's no food present to muffle the sound. Loud growling noises don't necessarily mean that a person is hungry, however, but simply that the digestive system is active and the stomach is empty.

IS CHOCOLATE ADDICTIVE?

Chocolate is a psychoactive food (ie one that's capable of affecting mood and/or behaviour) made from a variety of the cacao tree called the Theobroma, a Greek word meaning 'food of the gods'. It has been suggested by some that chocolate can be addictive, and, indeed, the fact that it contains an array of complex chemicals might support this claim. For instance, chocolate contains a compound called anandamide, which is a cannabinoid (as is marijuana), as well as chemicals that inhibit the breakdown of cannabinoids – which are, in fact, produced naturally by the body and synthesised in the brain. Chocolate contains compounds that make this chemical remain in the bloodstream for longer, which some people cite as the reason for any chemical dependency on chocolate.

Chocolate also contains caffeine, a stimulant that increases the consumer's sense of satisfaction and floods the brain with endorphins, which act something like opiates, reducing a person's sensitivity to pain and producing a similar effect to that of morphine. It also contains quantities of tryptophan, a mood regulator that enhances serotonin function.

Also appearing on the list of chocolate's ingredients is phenylethylamine, a chemical that is said to produce a high similar to that produced by taking amphetamines. It occurs naturally in the brain and releases dopamine, which promotes feelings of euphoria, such as those that peak during sexual orgasm. Some claim that eating chocolate produces a milder form of this feeling, although others suggest that the chemical is digested before it reaches the brain.

Chocolate also contains theobromine, a chemical that is toxic to horses, dogs and parrots when consumed in large amounts because they are unable to metabolise it, leading to heart attacks, internal bleeding and death. However, chocolate has been proven to be beneficial to human health as it contains antioxidants, which help to protect the body against cancer and heart problems.

WHY DO PEOPLE SOMETIMES SEE 'STARS'?

Sometimes, when people physically exert themselves or stand up quickly after sitting or bending over, they see little spots of light moving in front of them. This phenomenon can also occur after a blow to the head and is generally referred to as seeing 'stars'. It is caused by a condition known as *posterior vitreous detachment* (which often also results in blurred vision), whereby the vitreous humor – the jellylike fluid that fills the eyeball – detaches from the optic nerve, an action that the brain perceives as flashes of light. In most cases, this is only temporary and normal vision is restored in a few seconds, but it is more common in elderly people, whose vitreous humor has degenerated and partially liquefied. In some cases, the retina can fully detach and the flashes become permanent.

Low blood pressure can also cause flashes,

especially when someone changes position quickly. In this case, the flashes are caused by a lack of blood flow to the visual areas of the brain.

IS USING SUN BEDS BAD FOR YOUR SKIN?

Many people use sun beds (also known as solariums) to attain a tan all year round. They operate by producing ultra-violet radiation, which darkens a pigment in the skin called melanin to provide a tan. Sun beds produce mainly UV-A rays, along with some UV-B rays. For years scientists thought that UV-A radiation didn't damage the skin, but it's now known that these rays are harmful and result in long-term damage, penetrating the deep layers of the skin to destroy the collagen and elastin fibres, which causes the skin to age more rapidly and results in wrinkles and freckles on the skin. The rays can also bring about an increased risk of contracting skin cancer.

While the UV-A undoubtedly provide a tan, they don't stimulate skin cells to produce a thicker epidermis, unlike UV-B rays from the sun, which means that the tan from UV-A rays doesn't provide any extra protection from further exposure to ultra-violet radiation. In fact, by prematurely aging the skin, UV-A rays damage the regenerative cells in the skin, causing it to be more susceptible to the more harmful UV-B rays when the skin is later exposed to the sun.

It has recently been suggested that using sun beds might be addictive, in that the rays they use increase the production rate of endorphins in the brain, providing the user with a pleasurable sensation.

Because sun beds have been in use for only a few years, the extent of the damage they cause is not yet fully known. However, skin specialists claim that no tan is healthy and that sun beds should be avoided, especially by people with fair complexions.

HOW DOES VIAGRA WORK?

Viagra is the trade name of the drug sildenafil citrate, which is manufactured by the pharmaceutical company Pfizer, and is used by men who have difficulty getting or maintaining an erect penis. The drug was initially developed to treat heart conditions, but the effects it had on the penis were noticed during the testing stages and the company introduced a shift in marketing.

In healthy men, sexual arousal brings about an increase in the rate of blood flow to the penis, resulting in an erection. This increase in blood flow is brought about by the release into the penis of nitric oxide, which stimulates an enzyme that works to increase the levels of a chemical called cGMP, a chemical that in turn relaxes the muscles and arteries in the penis and allows the blood to flow freely. If the nerves or blood vessels in the penis aren't working properly, this process is inhibited. Viagra acts to reduce the effects of another chemical in the body that degrades cGMP, an action that results in a greater amount of cGMP in the body, leading to an erection. For Viagra to work, the man must be sexually aroused so that the nitric oxide and cGMP levels are released in the first place.

Viagra has a number of minor side-effects, such as headaches, sneezing, priapism (prolonged erections) and heart palpitations, while in extreme cases it can contribute to strokes or even death.

WHY IS A DOLLAR CALLED A 'BUCK' IN THE US?

In the United States and other countries where the unit of currency is the dollar, the slang term 'buck' is often used in its place. The most popular theory of the word's origin is that it derives from the American Indian bartering of goods in the eighteenth century. At that time, the hide of a male deer – buckskin – was a common bartering item. The term was later shortened to 'buck' and, as the bartering system was gradually replaced with a system of monetary exchange, the word came to be a reference for a dollar. Some people argue, however, that a dollar wasn't referred to as a buck until well after the bartering system had been replaced, also claiming that one buckskin was worth far more than one dollar.

Another possible origin of the word 'buck' is as an early gambling term. When gambling was first practised in America, a marker was used to determine whose turn it was to deal, and this marker was known as a 'buck', because it was usually a buck knife, with a handle fashioned from buck horn. A silver dollar was said to be used later as the marker, but the term 'buck' remained.

It has also been claimed that a buck was a term given to a young black slave to be traded for goods, although this is thought unlikely and it is generally believed that the word 'buck' has nothing to do with slavery.

WHAT ARE RAINBOWS AND HOW ARE THEY FORMED?

A rainbow is a large band of adjacent stripes of various colours that forms in an arc when the sun shines on water suspended in the atmosphere. It displays the spectrum of colours, with red on the outside, then heading inwards through orange, yellow, green, blue and indigo to violet.

These colours appear through the prismatic quality of water (usually raindrops), which breaks up and refracts the sunlight at an array of angles, depending on its intensity. The angle of the most intense light is between 40 and 42 degrees, which is why a rainbow takes the form of an arc.

For a rainbow to be visible, the observer must be in a position between the suspended water in front and the sun behind, which explains why rainbows are seen most often in mornings or afternoons, when the sun is low in the sky. If the sun is too high, it won't be behind the observer and no rainbow will be seen. Because of the necessary alignment of the sun and the rain, a rainbow can be seen from only one side.

A rainbow doesn't actually exist in the sky; it's a visual artifice personal to the observer. Each person sees a different personal rainbow at a different position in the sky, depending on where he or she is standing.

Since a rainbow must face the observer squarely, it's not possible to approach the sides or back of a rainbow, and this is probably how the expression 'searching for a pot of gold at the end of the rainbow' came about: it can never be found, and the phrase signifies a futile search.

DOES SHAVED HAIR GROW BACK THICKER AND DARKER?

It's often said that cutting or shaving hair on the head or body makes it grow back faster, thicker and darker than it originally was. This is not true.

The amount of hair on the human body, as well as its growth rate and colour, are determined by the individual hair follicles. These aren't affected or stimulated by shaving, nor does shaving promote the growth of additional hair follicles. The diameter of the hair follicles is also unaffected. In fact, the thickness and darkness of an individual's hair, as well as its growth rate, are determined by his or her genetics. The live part of the hair is actually underneath the skin, in the follicle, and so shaving or cutting has no impact on it.

The myth that hair grows back thicker and darker after shaving probably stems from the fact that the shorter hair at the early stages of regrowth seems tougher than longer hair. This is due to the fact that each hair is usually thicker at the base, where it has been cut, than the ends, which taper off naturally. This makes the hair blunter and more noticeable than the original hair, which had a much finer tip. In time, the cut hair will grow to be the same thickness and density as it was at its previous length.

WHY ARE PEOPLE'S EYES DIFFERENT COLOURS?

The coloured part of the human eye, surrounding the black pupil, is called the iris, a word deriving from the personification of the rainbow in Greek mythology. The colour of the iris is usually brown, blue, green or hazel.

The colour of the iris is provided by a pigment called melanin, which is also present in the body's hair and skin, although this is of a slightly different type. The melanin in the iris is yellow-brown to dark brown in colour, and the amount of melanin in a person's irises will determine their eye colour – for instance, a person with a high level of melanin will have brown eyes, while someone with less melanin in their irises will have blue eyes. People whose skin and hair are dark tend to have more melanin and darker eyes than people whose skin and hair are fair.

It was originally thought that eye colour was determined by one specific gene, but it is now believed that a number of genes are involved. The genes that cause brown eyes are dominant, so, if one parent has brown eyes and the other parent has blue eyes, the child is more likely (though not certain) to have brown eyes. It is, however, possible for a brown-eyed parent to produce a child with blue eyes if the parent's eye colour is the result of carrying recessive blue-eyed genes as well as the dominant brown-eyed genes. In addition, some blue-eyed babies' eyes darken as their levels of melanin increase with age.

It is possible, although rare, for a person to have different levels of melanin in each eye, a condition called *heterochromia iridium*, which results in each eye being a different colour. This condition can be inherited or can result from an alteration of one of the relevant genes. Alexander the Great had this condition, as does David Bowie. A similar condition, *heterochromia iridis*, manifests itself as a variety of colours within one eye.

WHERE DO FLIES AND MOSQUITOES GO IN WINTER?

During the summer months, flies and mosquitoes are abundant, but, when winter arrives, they seem to disappear magically until the temperature warms up again. But why? And where do they go?

Some of these insects hibernate through the cold winter months in dark and damp places, such as in logs or under houses. When the weather warms, the females become active, feed and lay eggs. Similarly, some flies are programmed to become dormant before the cold weather sets in – ie they *diapause*. The rise in temperature breaks the dormancy.

Other insects simply don't survive the cold weather and die. These insects lay their eggs in summer and, when the winter arrives, the adults die and the eggs freeze. In spring and summer, the eggs thaw and hatch to produce the next generation.

Some bush flies die out completely in the colder

areas but thrive in warmer climes, and in the summer they are blown from the warmer areas to repopulate the colder areas, where they breed again.

Some other species of insects, such as the monarch butterfly and certain crop pests, migrate to warmer areas during the cold months, only to return when the temperature increases.

WHY DO PEOPLE STICK OUT THEIR TONGUE WHILE CONCENTRATING?

It is quite common for people inadvertently to stick their tongue out of their mouth when concentrating intently on a mechanical task, such as trying to fix a recalcitrant piece of machinery. The reason why the tongue often protrudes without the person's knowledge is rooted in the fact that different areas of the brain have different functions while some areas have multiple functions.

The frontal lobe of the brain's left hemisphere is responsible for co-ordinating the complex muscular actions of the mouth and tongue. The same area of the brain deals with higher intellectual functions, such as concentrating, problem-solving and judgement, which means that, when someone is concentrating on something or trying to solve a problem, they're engaging the hemisphere of the brain that's also used for processing the motor activity of the tongue. The two activities – concentrating and controlling the tongue – carried out at the same time cause interference in the brain, which sends impulses to the tongue, telling it to poke out in order to keep it still, suspending its motor activity while the thought processes are being undertaken. Because the person is concentrating so much, he or she generally doesn't notice that his or her tongue is protruding.

For the same reasons, quite often when a person is thinking intently, he or she will walk more slowly. Again, this is because the same area of the brain that's used for thinking controls motor skills, such as walking, and, by walking slower, the person is minimising the body's movements and the interference this would otherwise cause for the more complex thought processes.

HOW DID THE SAYING 'DRESSED TO THE NINES' ORIGINATE?

This expression refers to someone who is well dressed or formally dressed. There are a number of explanations for its origin, which is still thought to be uncertain. One possible source is tailors, who once used nine yards of fabric to make the best suits, while another is Greek mythology, specifically the nine Muses. It might also stem from attaining a standard of nine out of ten, alluding to near perfection.

Another popular theory is that the source of the phrase can be found with the British Army's Ninety-ninth Regiment of Foot, who were renowned for being well dressed, while other regiments were always trying to equal the standard of 'the nines'. However, this regiment was in existence during the 1850s and the phrase existed well before that time.

The first recorded usage of the expression is in Robert Burns's 'Poem on Pastoral Poetry' of 1793, specifically in the line 'Thou paints auld Nature to the nines'.

A similar saying to 'dressed to the nines' is 'the whole nine yards'. Like the former phrase, there are a number of conflicting theories concerning its origin and, similarly, it's likely that the truth will never be known.

WHAT CAUSES 'RINGING' IN THE EARS?

From time to time, many experience a ringing or buzzing noise in the ears when there is no external sound source. This is due to a condition called Tinnitus, which affects the nervous system. The volume and type of the noise varies from person to person and depends on what is causing the tinnitus, while its severity can range from a mild annoyance to extreme pain.

Tinnitus can be caused by a number of things, such

as a head injury or the experiencing of a sudden loud noise. Depression, stress, a build-up of ear wax, problem teeth and certain drugs can also cause it.

There are two types of tinnitus. With objective tinnitus (often known as 'real' tinnitus), the sound can be heard by a third person, usually with the help of a stethoscope, and might be caused by deformation of the blood vessels or a spasming of the muscles in the ear. Subjective tinnitus – also known as 'false' tinnitus – is the more common variety and is perceived only by the person who is experiencing it. It's thought to be as a result of some type of derangement in areas of the nervous system that are involved with hearing.

For most people, tinnitus usually lasts for only a few seconds or minutes, but it can be prolonged and even permanent. In severe cases, it can be very disruptive to a person's life and is sometimes incurable. To combat its effects, people often wear electronic tinnitus maskers, which are worn like a hearing aid and act to mask the noise. Psychological counselling is also employed in chronic cases.

WHAT ARE THE ORIGINS OF THE HAMBURGER AND THE HOTDOG?

The hamburger and the hotdog are everyday fast-food items that are sold in many countries around the world, particularly the United States. Even today, the origins of these foodstuffs remain uncertain.

The word *hamburger* comes from the German city of Hamburg, where the food first became popular. Some people believe that German immigrants then brought the hamburger to the United States in the nineteenth century, while others say that it was invented by Charlie Nagreen at the Outagamie County Fair in Seymour, Wisconsin, in 1885. Nagreen supposedly sold fried meatballs at the fair, but his customers had trouble carrying them and so he flattened them inside a bun and called them hamburgers. Meanwhile, an establishment called Louis' Lunch in New Haven, Connecticut, also claims to have invented the hamburger. The popular view, however, is that the first proper hamburgers in buns were made in 1904 at the St Louis World's Fair. Despite the origins of the hamburger, it became world renowned in the 1950s with the opening of the fast-food chain McDonald's.

Like the hamburger, the hotdog is said to have originated at the 1904 St Louis World's Fair, when a Bavarian named Anton Feuchtwanger apparently lent his customers gloves with which to hold hot sausages. When the gloves weren't returned, he employed his brother – a baker – to provide buns instead.

Another theory is that hotdogs were invented by Harry Stevens at the New York Polo Grounds in

1901, when, on a cold day, he bought dachshund sausages and sold them in warm buns to the New York Giants fans. A sports cartoonist on the day, Tad Dorgan, drew a cartoon of it and, unsure how to spell 'dachshund', wrote, 'Hot dog!' While this is commonly believed to be where the term originated, similar items were sold in Germany well before that time, and it is said that St Louis Browns owner Chris von der Ahe sold them at his baseball park in 1880.

WHAT IS MENSTRUAL SYNCHRONY AND DOES IT EXIST?

Menstrual synchrony is the phenomenon where the menstrual cycles of women sharing an environment for some time coincide. This can occur among mothers and daughters, or among females sharing dormitories, or even among women who work together. The phenomenon was first studied in 1971 and, while the reason for its existence is largely unknown (and its existence is even questioned by some), some scientists believe it to be caused by pheromones – a type of scent cue – that are expelled from women to indicate and encourage menstruation of the whole group.

It's thought that women expel these pheromones because of a trait that initially developed in our ancestors. One theory is that, because men reproduced with a number of females, it was important for the cycles to be in line in order to ensure reproductive efficiency, from the male's perspective. It's also thought that women might have cycled together for the benefit of the community, as it meant that babies would be born at around the same time, so the women in a tribe could support and help each other; for instance, if one mother were unable to feed her baby, there would have been another nearby to do so. Similarly, some people believe that women who menstruated together would have joined emotionally and guided each other through the process. While these community reasons no longer exist in modern society, they are still instinctual in women.

Critics claim that menstrual synchrony does not exist and that the women who participated in such surveys either misremembered the exact dates or were influenced by the answers of others, or that any similarities in menstruation times were merely coincidental, due to the limited number of days available in a monthly cycle. They also criticise the methodology behind the studies, which they accuse of biasing the results, and say that menstrual synchrony is impossible with some women whose cycles differ in length.

DOES WATER PRESSURE PLUMMET DURING TELEVISION ADVERTISEMENTS IN THE US SUPER BOWL?

It has been rumoured for years that the televising of the Super Bowl football tournament in the United States has an adverse effect on water supplies and pressures in the country. Supposedly, because so many people watch the game on television, during the advertisements there is either a severe drop in water pressure or a water shortage as a large fraction of the country's population uses the toilet.

This claim is thought to have originated from an announcement from a New York environmental department advising people to stagger their toilet breaks during the game so as to not place the city's water supply under too much pressure. It was later claimed that this wasn't a serious concern and that the announcement was made to create media hype. Indeed, after the game it was acknowledged that there was no noticeable impact on the city's water supply.

It is has been accepted by government authorities, however, that such issues affecting the nation's water supply have occurred. During the screening of the final episode of *M*A*S*H* in 1983, the drop in pressure of the New York City water supply during the advertisements apparently resulted in a water surge. The same result is said to have been caused by other television broadcasts, such as the annual Academy Awards and the 1969 moon landing.

Authorities claim that these surges of water last for only a matter of minutes and don't cause dramatic problems. Pumps and other devices in the water system can rectify any minor imbalances and bring the water pressure quickly back to normal.

WHY DO GOOD RESTAURANTS ALLOW YOU TO TASTE WINE BEFORE BUYING IT?

After a sommelier in an expensive restaurant has shown a party host the label of an unopened bottle of wine, so that they can ensure it's the correct bottle, he will often then pour a tiny amount of wine into the host's glass before filling the glasses of the other customers at the table. The host will then normally swirl the wine around in the glass, smell it and then taste it. If content, he will indicate to the waiter that the wine is acceptable. The glasses are then filled – clockwise, with ladies first and the host's glass last. Sometimes the waiter will offer the cork of the bottle to the host so that he can smell it before offering him a taste of the wine itself.

Despite popular belief, this tasting ritual is not designed so that the host can send back a bottle of wine of which he or she is not particularly fond; it's solely to determine that the wine is still drinkable and hasn't been spoiled, or 'corked', which is the only situation in which the wine might be rejected. Spoiled or corked wine is that which has been oxidised, which means that it has been exposed to air, usually through a flaw in the cork. Corked wine often tastes mouldy or of vinegar.

WHAT IS THE HISTORY OF ST VALENTINE'S DAY?

Valentine's Day occurs on 14 February and is celebrated by many people by giving flowers and cards to their romantic partners. The day is named after St Valentine, the patron saint of romance and one of the three saints recognised by the Catholic Church with that name, each of whom was martyred on 14 February.

Legend has it that the day is named after the priest named St Valentine who was alive in Rome during the third century. Emperor Claudius II believed that unmarried men were more likely to enlist in the army, so he outlawed marriage for young men. Incensed by this, St Valentine performed secret marriages for young lovers but was caught out, imprisoned and executed on 14 February 270. It's said that, while in prison, St Valentine fell in love with the daughter of a jailer who visited him, and that before he was killed he wrote her a note, which he signed, 'From your

Valentine,' which has survived to become a common expression today.

The feast of St Valentine was declared by Pope Gelasius I in around 496 to occur on 14 February. Each year, the women would write love letters on that day and place them in an urn. The men would pick a letter from the urn and pursue the note's author over the course of the following year.

St Valentine's Day remained a Church holiday until 1969, when Pope Paul VI removed it from the Church calendar.

WHAT ARE COMPUTER VIRUSES AND HOW DO THEY WORK?

A computer virus is a small program that is distributed between computers via removable media, such as floppy disks or CD-ROMs, or the Internet. In many ways, it is similar to a biological virus, piggybacking on to real programs and passing from computer to computer, spreading the infection, while it can also spread to other programs within the host computer. As each program is launched, the virus launches with it, infecting any other programs currently in operation. If an infected program or document is then sent to another computer and launched or opened, the cycle continues and the virus spreads. As it does so, it often attacks the host computer, causing it to send emails containing copies of itself (thus further spreading the infection), corrupting files or even deleting all the data from the computer.

The first computer virus is said to have been written in 1982, and today they come in a variety of forms. The most common is the aforementioned email virus, which reaches a computer while attached to an email message and, when the email is opened, automatically launches itself, whereupon it replicates by sending copies of itself to everyone else in the host user's address book. An example of this type of virus was the 'I Love You' email virus in 2000.

Another kind of computer infection is a worm, which in many ways is similar to a virus. A worm will scan a computer network, searching for security holes via which it can replicate itself in other networks.

More sophisticated viruses, meanwhile, load on to a computer's memory and run in the background as long as the computer is switched on, which gives them more opportunity to spread by infecting any programs that are run. As most computers are linked to the Internet, this makes the spreading of viruses rife, as many people might have access to and open the same programs.

In most countries, the creation of viruses is illegal. It's thought that they're created by vandals who enjoy watching and marvelling at the destruction they cause, before later bragging about their achievements to other virus writers. Fortunately, all modern desktop computers are equipped with security devices, such as Firewall programs and virus scanners, to detect and block viruses.

WHY DOES ALCOHOL CAUSE PEOPLE TO URINATE SO MUCH?

The reason why people urinate so frequently while drinking alcohol is because it is a diuretic – ie a drug that increases the amount of urine produced by the kidneys. Caffeine, too, is a diuretic.

Alcohol's diuretic effect works by preventing the blood-regulation function of vasopressin, an anti-diuretic hormone that acts on the kidneys, compelling them to concentrate the urine by increasing the reabsorption of water. A decrease in vasopressin therefore reduces the amount of water reabsorbed by the kidneys, resulting in the production of larger amounts of urine. This diuretic effect draws water from the body and causes a person to urinate more fluid than they imbibe.

The diuretic effect (or diuresis) is caused not by the volume of liquid drunk but by the alcohol content of the drink. A shot of spirits will generally cause a person to generate as much urine as they would if they drank a pint of beer.

WHEN WAS LIPSTICK INVENTED AND WHAT WAS ITS ORIGINAL PURPOSE?

Lipstick has been in existence for thousands of years, first appearing near Babylon in the city of Ur in 3000 BC. In Ancient Egypt, Cleopatra wore lipstick made from crushed red beetles, while the women of Ancient Greece also painted their lips. There are numerous accounts of it being manufactured in ancient times from dyes extracted from certain plants.

Elizabeth I was the main instigator of lipstick in England during the Middle Ages, after which it didn't become prevalent again until after the French Revolution. The wearing of lipstick was previously thought to be uncouth, and any woman using it was considered a fake attempting to capture her lost youth. In fact, in 1770 a law was proposed to the British parliament that any marriage could be annulled where it could be shown that the woman had used cosmetics prior to the wedding day. If she lured a man into matrimony through her use of cosmetics, she could be tried for witchcraft.

In modern times, lipstick is of course commonplace and is currently made from oils, fats, pigments and waxes, while moisturisers and sunscreen are also found as ingredients.

Some scientists believe that the original purpose of lipstick was to arouse men. The lips are said to replicate the female genitalia, and lipstick augmented their appearance and mimicked the genitals in a stimulated state. The red colour of lipstick supposedly gives the impression of the genitals being in this aroused state and engorged with blood.

WHY DOES THE SOUND OF SCRAPING FINGERNAILS MAKE PEOPLE CRINGE?

For most people, one of the most hideous sounds is that of fingernails scraping down a blackboard. But why should this be so? Scientists have conducted many experiments and undertaken much research to answer this question. After each experiment, they have concluded that the sound of fingernails scraping in such a way is the most excruciating noise for the human ear.

To determine what makes the sound so terrible, scientists have filtered out different portions of the sound. They found that, when the high-pitched portion is removed, the sound is equally unbearable, but that, when the low-pitched portion is removed, the sound doesn't make people cringe. This led them to the conclusion that it was the lower frequencies of the sound that people couldn't stand. Still, this didn't explain why this should be the case.

Researchers now believe that people's objection to the noise is inherited from a common primate ancestor and is hardwired into our brains. They found that the scraping-fingernail noise is very similar to the warning cry of certain monkeys, which suggests that our response to the noise is an instinctual reflex to potential danger. If this is indeed the case, it's a reflex that we've had for tens of thousands of years.

WHAT IS THE DIFFERENCE BETWEEN A HURRICANE AND A TYPHOON?

A tropical cyclone is a series of storms in which winds are sustained at levels of at least 73mph, taking the form of a mass of air containing these storms, spiralling around a low-pressure centre. The centre of the air mass is called the eye, where the winds are calm and the sky clear. The more powerful the tropical cyclone, the smaller its eye. Tropical cyclones can cause significant damage to towns and vegetation by tearing through objects or causing flooding from excess rain.

A hurricane and a typhoon are different terms for a tropical cyclone, and where the cyclone is formed will determine which term is used: when they occur in the Western hemisphere in the Atlantic Ocean, the Gulf of Mexico or the Caribbean Sea, they are called hurricanes; when they occur in the north Pacific Ocean, west of the International Date Line, they are called typhoons; and in the southwest Pacific Ocean and most other parts of the Indian Ocean, they are known as tropical cyclones or cyclonic storms. Certain countries also have specific names for the storms: in the Philippines they are called Bagyo, in Mexico they are called Chubasco, and in Haiti they are called Taino.

Generally speaking, typhoons tend to be more powerful than hurricanes because the water they contain is about 2°C warmer in the tropical Pacific Ocean and warmer water provides a cyclone with more energy. Because of this difference in temperature, while the hurricane season runs from June to November, the typhoon season runs from May to December.

HOW DID THE WORD 'COCKTAIL' ORIGINATE FOR SOME ALCOHOLIC DRINKS?

A cocktail is an alcoholic drink that comprises a number of ingredients that are mixed or shaken together. There are hundreds of different concoctions and they are often sweet, colourful and interestingly named, such as the Grasshopper, the Rusty Nail, Sex on the Beach and the Hummingbird.

Like many words and phrases, there are a number of explanations for the origins of the word 'cocktail'. While it's likely that the correct one will never be known, it's commonly believed that the first written reference to the word was in an 1806 edition of *The Balance and Columbian Repository*, published in New York, which provided a description of a cocktail.

Some think that the word derived from a drink known as 'cock-ale', which in the eighteenth century was given to anger fighting cocks or to the patrons who attended the cockfights. Others believe it is a compound deriving from a name for an old American tap (a cock) and the dregs of a barrel (known as the tail). Another explanation is that publicans customarily placed a feather from a cock's tail into alcoholic drinks to warn of their alcoholic content, while yet another is that the word may have come from the French word *coquetel*, which was a mixed drink served to French officers during the American Revolution. It's also said that the name is derived from a particular bar in America where drinks were served out of a ceramic container shaped like a rooster (cock) that had a tap in the tail.

Other theories are that the word derives from a term used in second-century Rome, or from an old medical practice of using a cock's tail to apply throat medicine. There is also a reference to an alcoholic drink being strong enough to 'cock the tail' of a bob-tailed horse, known as a 'cocktailed horse'.

Probably the best-known origin, however, is from

an eighteenth-century American innkeeper named Betsy Flanagan who stole chickens from her British neighbour and cooked them for her patrons. After the meal, she would mix some drinks and place a feather in each of them. At this display, one French customer yelled in delight, 'Vive le cocktail!'

WHY IS IT THOUGHT THAT BLONDE WOMEN HAVE MORE FUN?

For centuries, men have generally tended to prefer women who have blonde hair. In Ancient Greece, for instance, blonde hair was associated with Aphrodite, the goddess of love and beauty. This love of the blonde continued in the times of the Roman Empire, when dark-haired women would buy light-coloured wigs made from the hair of Germanic people. Later, in mid-twentieth-century Nazi Germany, blonde people were taken as being members of the Aryan people (ie not Jewish) and seen as superior, and in jazz-age America, during the golden age of cinema, blonde women were also favoured for Hollywood productions.

Blonde hair dyes for women are five times more popular than any other colour. Even in modern society, women have been culturally conditioned to believe that blonde hair is desirable.

Blonde hair in women is caused by their hair having greater amounts of pale pigment than dark pigment, which is why men tend to have darker hair, having greater levels of dark pigmentation than women do. This lighter colouring is therefore subconsciously associated with femininity. Blonde hair is also a characteristic of female children, giving it an association with youthfulness, and it's therefore thought that blonde hair on women evokes paternal feelings in men.

As women age, decreasing levels of the female hormone oestrogen causes their hair to become darker, among other things. Because of this, it is believed that men subconsciously associate blonde hair with high fertility.

The fact that blonde women are seen as youthful, feminine and fertile often leads men to find them more desirable, resulting in them being pursued by men more frequently than women of other hair colours. This in turn leads to the perception that blonde women are always out having a good time and to the expression 'blondes have more fun'.

WHY DO PEOPLE GET DIZZY IF SPUN AROUND?

When a person spins repeatedly in circles, a sensation of dizziness or vertigo will often result. This is caused because the hair-like sensory nerve cells in the inner ear send incorrect signals to the brain.

The body senses its position and its motion through the vestibular system, which is contained in the upper part of the inner ear and consists of canals that contain the hair-like sensory nerve cells, as well as a fluid called endolymph, which, because of inertia, resists any change in motion. When we spin around, the endolymph lags behind and stimulates the hair cells to signal to the brain that the head is spinning. When the endolymph starts to move at the same rate as that at which you're spinning, it no longer stimulates the hair cells and the brain adapts to the motion. When the spinning stops, however, the endolymph carries on moving, and this motion again stimulates the hair cells, which fire signals to the brain, which in turn interprets these erroneous messages as signifying that spinning is still occurring, causing dizziness. Once the endolymph stops moving, the signals stops and the brain realises that the spinning has ceased. The dizziness then ceases.

After spinning around in one direction, if a person then reverses directions, the dizziness isn't as acute, because the change in direction helps to stop the endolymph from moving, the two directions of spinning cancelling each other out.

WHY IS THE PIRATE FLAG CALLED THE 'JOLLY ROGER'?

The Jolly Roger is the name given to the traditional flag hoisted on pirate ships, comprising a white skull and crossed bones on a black background, and the source of its name has been debated for many years. One theory is that the name is from a term used many years ago for the leader of a group of Asian pirates, who was called 'Ali Raja' (meaning 'king of sea'), and that English pirates stole and corrupted the name.

The most popular explanation for the flag's name, however, is that it derives from the French term 'jolie rouge' (meaning 'pretty red'), which referred to a red flag flown by some pirates in the Caribbean in the seventeenth century. The flag symbolised blood and indicated that the pirates who sailed under it were ruthless and would kill anyone they encountered. For this reason, a red flag was feared much more than a black flag. The name was subsequently used for the black flag with the skull and crossed bones, which first appeared in about 1700.

While the French derivation of the name is the most widely accepted, it is believed that the correct etymological source of the flag's assignation is from the name 'Old Roger', a nickname of the Devil.

WHY DOES THE PENIS SHRINK WHEN IT'S COLD?

In cold weather or water, a man's penis will often retract and reduce considerably in size. This phenomenon is sometimes referred to as 'shrinkage', and it occurs for a number of reasons, primarily that of temperature regulation. The testicles are contained in the scrotum and suspended away from the body, owing to the fact that sperm can be produced only when conditions are slightly cooler than the core temperature of the body. The temperature range at which sperm can be produced is very narrow, varying by only a couple of degrees, and when the environment gets too cold the scrotum retracts, drawing the testicles closer to the body to increase their temperature. As the penis is attached to the scrotum, this retraction pulls up the penis along with it.

A sufficiently steep drop in temperature will also prompt the body to reduce the amount of blood circulating to the extremities and appendages, and concentrate blood flow in the core of the body in order to protect the vital organs. As the size of the penis is affected greatly by the amount of blood that it receives, when a drop in temperature causes a reduction in the amount of blood that reaches it, the penis shrivels and decreases in size.

The penis can also reduce in size when a man is startled or frightened – again because the body retracts the scrotum to the body for maximum protection, hauling the penis in with it.

IS CAESAR SALAD NAMED AFTER JULIUS CAESAR?

The traditional Caesar salad is popular throughout the Western world. It's made from lettuce, croutons, garlic, lemon juice, olive oil, eggs, Worcestershire sauce and Parmesan cheese, while it also often includes bacon, anchovies, tomato and avocado. Many people believe that it was invented by and named after the Roman emperor Julius Caesar, but this is a fallacy; there is no connection between the dish and Julius Caesar. In fact, the dish was invented in 1924 in Tijuana, Mexico, by a restaurateur named Caesar Cardini, who was fervently against the inclusion of anchovies in the dish, maintaining that the Worcestershire sauce added a sufficiently fishy flavour.

A number of stories exist as to what first prompted Cardini to make the dish. One is that it was created for the Prince of Wales, who was stranded in Tijuana because of bad weather and Cardini was forced to concoct a dish with some leftovers he had in the kitchen. A second theory is that it was made for a group of Hollywood stars at the end of a long party.

WHAT IS SNOT AND WHY IS IT SOMETIMES GREEN?

Snot is a slang term for mucus, a thin and slippery material comprising mucins and inorganic salts suspended in water that's produced by the mucous membranes inside the nose. It serves to moisten and protect the nose and throat while also trapping inhaled foreign matter, keeping it in the nose and thus preventing dangerous particles and germs from reaching the lungs, where they could cause damage. Mucus surrounds any foreign matter that is trapped and dries around it, producing a hardened piece of snot.

Mucus production is normal and healthy, but increased production in the respiratory tract is often a sign of a disease, such as the common cold.

When snot appears green or yellow, this is usually because the body has a bacterial infection, causing it to produce thick mucus containing pus excreted by the bacteria. When the body's immune system detects the infection, it produces an enzyme called myeloperoxidase, which kills the bacteria in the mucus and expels it through the nose. The green colour is caused by the pus from the bacteria, as well as an ion in the myeloperoxidase.

The nose produces around a cupful of snot every day.

DOES SPEAKING TO PLANTS ENCOURAGE THEM TO GROW?

Many people maintain that talking to plants, and exposing them to melodious sounds generally, encourages them to grow and promotes health. Indeed, albums have been recorded specifically for the purpose of invigorating plant growth.

A number of scientific studies have been conducted in an attempt to prove this. One study found that ultrasonic vibrations stimulated the production of hormones in plants and encouraged growth, while others have discovered that sounds that fall within the range of human hearing also led to increased growth.

There have also been studies carried out to determine which type of music produces the best results, suggesting that classical music made plants healthier whereas loud rock music was detrimental to their health. One such study indicated that extremely loud noises increased the germination rate of some plants.

It was suggested as early as the nineteenth century that plants were capable of emotions and were likely to be healthier if they received a lot of attention. It has also been claimed that, while they evidently can't understand the spoken word, plants are capable of understanding the meaning behind speech. Charles

Darwin even compared certain characteristics of primates with those of plants.

Proponents of the theory that talking to plants encourages growth argue that such action involves respiration, providing the plants with extra carbon dioxide, which they need in order to grow. In addition, if a plant's owner speaks to it on a regular basis, he or she is likely to notice things wrong with it – such as pest infestation – and can then deal with them before they cause a serious problem.

Despite the many studies and theories on the topic, there is thought to be no scientific evidence to suggest that playing music or talking to plants will increase their growth rate or make them healthier.

WHY IS A RABBIT'S FOOT CONSIDERED GOOD LUCK?

It is a long-held superstition that the bearer of a rabbit's foot will receive good luck. The original superstition was that it was only the rabbit's left hind foot that brought the luck, and it had to be rubbed in order to release the luck.

The origins of this superstition date back to Western Europe in 600 BC, a time when people considered rabbits to be sacred animals, believing that man was descended from animals such as rabbits and that spirits inhabited the animals' bodies. As rabbits spent a lot of time underground, the Celts later believed that dark, diabolical underground spirits lived in rabbits. The prolific reproduction rate of rabbits also led to them being adopted as a symbol of fertility, prosperity and health. The speed of the animal, and the fact that its hind legs went ahead of its forelegs when it ran, brought about the idea that rabbits and their feet were a source of protective magic.

Because the rabbit was so highly revered, any part of the rabbit received equal honour. It's thought that its foot was selected as the good-luck charm because it dried quickly and its small size made it easy to carry.

HOW DO FLIES LAND AND WALK UPSIDE DOWN?

As most people know, flies are able to land upside-down and then stay there or even walk along. For many years, scientists believed that they approached a ceiling by flying normally and then, at the last second, performing a barrel-roll to land upside-down. In the 1950s, however, when scientists filmed flies landing, this myth was dispelled when they discovered that flies approach the ceiling using their normal method of flying and then, just prior to impact, extend their two front legs. These legs then attach to the ceiling and the fly swings its body up, like a trapeze artist, until its remaining four legs attach to the ceiling.

The fly is able to perform this manoeuvre because of its momentum, and also because of its short wings and strong mid-section wing muscles. Flies also have three groups of sensory organs, which determine their speed and position.

Once attached to a ceiling, a fly is then able to remain upside-down or walk along without falling. It's able to do this because its feet have spongy pads covered with a sticky glue-like substance that sticks the fly to the surface. The feet are also covered in hairs that the fly uses to hook into tiny grooves in the surface. It is thought that the pads on the feet might also be able to change shape to work as suction cups, affixing the fly to the surface.

In addition to helping the fly to walk upside-down and vertically, the sticky pads and hairy feet also make the fly an adept carrier of germs and disease.

WHAT MAKES PEOPLE GET SEASICK AND CARSICK?

Seasickness and carsickness are both forms of motion sickness, which can also occur during air travel and weightlessness.

Motion sickness is caused by conflicting signals from the ears and the eyes being sent to the brain. As described in 'Why Do People Get Dizzy If Spun Around?', the inner ear – which is responsible for maintaining a person's equilibrium – contains fluid called endolymph. When someone is in a moving car or boat, this fluid becomes agitated, causing nerve cells to send signals to the brain informing it that he or she is moving, while the signals from his or her eyes indicate that he or she is stationary. This conflict of signals between perceived movement and actual movement results in motion sickness.

The most common symptoms of motion sickness are nausea and vomiting. In fact, the word 'nausea' derives from the Greek word *naus*, meaning 'ship'. Unlike many illnesses, vomiting does not improve the sufferer's plight.

There are a number of ways of preventing or alleviating motion sickness. Fixing your eyes on distant objects can help because it makes the brain realise that movement is in fact taking place, which accords with the signals being sent to it by the ears. Reading a book is inadvisable, however, because this persuades the brain that you're stationary. Sitting facing forwards while travelling also helps, as does sitting in the front seat of a car, or the area of the vehicle that has the least amount of movement. Fresh air, a full stomach and frequent stops can also be helpful, as can closing the eyes and taking certain medications. It's also said that chewing on ginger reduces motion sickness.

The jerkier the movement, the more disruption is caused to the inner ear and the more pronounced the symptoms of motion sickness. Rough seas and windy roads should therefore be avoided.

WHAT IS THE HORIZON AND IS THE DISTANCE TO IT ALWAYS THE SAME?

The horizon is a distant line separating the sky from the Earth and is most noticeable at sea, where a person's line of sight to it is generally unimpeded. On land, the horizon is often obscured by natural or manmade objects.

An observer's distance to the horizon varies because of the curvature of the Earth and will depend on the observer's height above sea level, as well as his or her location on the planet. The distance to the horizon can be calculated approximately by multiplying the observer's elevation (in metres) by thirteen and then calculating the square root of this figure. For example, if a person were 3m above sea level, the horizon would be 6.25km away, whereas for a person at the top of a building 100m high, the horizon would be 36km away.

However, because the Earth is ellipsoidal (ie it's not a perfect sphere), it has a larger circumference near the equator. As a result, the northern horizon in the northern hemisphere is slightly further away than the southern horizon. The eastern and western horizons are equidistant yet slightly more distant than the southern and slightly closer than the northern. In the southern hemisphere, of course, the reverse of this is true.

WHY DO PREGNANT WOMEN GET MORNING SICKNESS?

Morning sickness is a specific type of nausea and vomiting suffered by women in the early stages of pregnancy, normally first occurring in the first month of pregnancy, and lasts until about the sixteenth week. It is most common soon after waking but can occur at any time of the day and is thought to affect between 50 and 85 per cent of pregnant women.

It's not known why pregnant women get morning sickness, although there are many theories. The most common is that, because levels of hormones – particularly oestrogen and progesterone – increase dramatically during pregnancy, this relaxes the muscles of the uterus in order to prevent early labour, while also possibly relaxing the stomach muscles and increasing the production of stomach acids. A low blood-sugar level during pregnancy is also cited by some as the cause of morning sickness, as is a vitamin B6 deficiency or an increase in stress and a heightened emotional state.

Another common suggestion for the malady's cause is an increased sensitivity to odours, the theory being that a pregnant woman smells things more acutely than other people, causing nausea. Food that isn't completely fresh or contains toxins is particularly offensive to pregnant women, and one of the first things that pregnant women detest is coffee, which contains many toxins, including caffeine. It is thought that this is a natural response of the woman's body, preventing her from eating foods that might harm her baby.

Connected to this theory is the fact that eating vegetables can sometimes cause morning sickness. Evolutionists believe that this is due to the fact that vegetables contain toxins that are produced to deter insects. While these toxins are generally harmless to humans, they can cause chromosomal and genetic damage in embryos, and so it is thought that morning sickness could be evidence of the body rejecting these vegetables and their toxins in order to protect the foetus. This might explain why pregnant women often find bitter foods like cauliflower and broccoli especially distasteful.

In order to prevent or alleviate morning sickness,

foods or smells that trigger the nausea should be avoided. Eating bland foods rather than those that are spicy or bitter is also suggested as a way of avoiding it, as is eating at regular intervals so that the stomach is never completely empty. Relaxation and plenty of sleep are also recommended.

WHAT IS THE ORIGIN OF THE TATTOO?

The word 'tattoo' is actually Tahitian in origin, meaning 'to mark', although the birthplace of the tattoo is a matter of some conjecture.

Some people believe that tattooing existed as early as 3300 BC, as the skin of a mummified Iceman was found to bear such markings. Egyptian mummies dating back to 2000 BC have also been found with tattoos.

In Ancient Greece, spies used tattooing as a form of communication, while the Ancient Romans tattooed slaves and criminals and some early Nordic people bore tattoos of their family crests. The Japanese, Chinese and many African peoples also used various forms of tattooing.

The Europeans discovered tattooing during their explorations of the south Pacific. In 1691, on his return to London, William Dampier brought with him a tattooed Polynesian, who was presented to people as a source of entertainment. Captain James

Cook also encountered tattooed people on his travels to this region in 1770.

The first modern tattoo shop was set up in Chatham Square, New York City, at around the turn of the twentieth century by a man named Samuel O'Reilly. In 1891, O'Reilly also patented the first electronic tattooing machine, a device whose operation was based on that of Thomas Edison's electric pen. Today's modern tattooing machine uses the same principle and takes the form of a hand-held electric tool that injects ink into the skin, moving a needle up and down at the rate of several hundred vibrations per minute. This needle penetrates the skin by about 1mm each time, injecting ink into the skin's dermis, the cells of which are stable and don't shed like those of the epidermis. The upshot of this is that the ink remains in the skin and the tattoo stays with its owner, with minimal fading, for life.

WHAT IS THE G SPOT AND WHERE IS IT?

The G spot is a small area in a woman's vagina that, when stimulated, is said to give her intense orgasms. It's named after its discoverer, Ernest Grafenberg, a German physician who conducted research on that area of the vagina in the 1950s. In recent years, scientists have conducted further research.

The G spot is said to be located on the upper front

vaginal wall, close to where the urethra joins the bladder. While its exact position can vary, it is commonly situated 2–3in inside the vagina, directly behind the pubic bone. It is the size of a small coin and has a spongy texture, distinguishing it from the otherwise smooth vaginal wall. Many women have difficulty in finding it, and some cannot find it at all.

The G spot is usually very sensitive and is capable of hardening and swelling. When pressure is applied to it, it can stimulate the need to urinate, and it might be the organ responsible for female ejaculation. One theory for the existence of this phenomenon is that during childbirth the head of the child pushes on the G spot, triggering the ejaculation, which lubricates the birth canal and helps with the final phase of birth.

Many people still maintain that the G spot doesn't exist, or that it doesn't contribute to orgasms in women. Others, meanwhile, claim that it is a part of the clitoris, the nerves of which penetrate deep below the surface.

HOW DO HUMMINGBIRDS HOVER?

The hummingbird is a small bird found only in the Americas, from Canada and Alaska to the Caribbean. It's extremely acrobatic, hovering in mid-air as it feeds on nectar from flowers, and is the only bird that can fly backwards, while it can also fly upside-down.

Some species – of which there are 330 – can reach flight speeds of 40kph almost instantly.

The hummingbird's ability to hover in mid-air stems from the rapid motion of its wings, which beat around eighty times each second. Unlike those of other birds, the hummingbird's wings move forwards and backwards instead of up and down, and each entire wing rotates in a figure-eight formation, the forward and backward strokes of the wing producing lift. The bird's name is derived from the humming noise produced by this rapid wing motion.

While it's undoubtedly effective, this unique flying technique is inefficient, and the hummingbird has the highest metabolism of any animal, with a heart rate approaching 500 beats per minute. This incredibly rapid metabolism is necessary to support the hummingbird's rapid wing beats and requires the bird to consume enormous quantities of food each day in order to stay alive.

WHAT CAUSES PEOPLE'S EARS TO POP?

Quite often, when people return to ground level after being in aeroplanes, under water or in an elevator, their ears pop. This sensation is caused by a rapid change in air pressure and occurs in order to equalise the pressure of the air between the middle ear and the ear canal. A great differential of air pressure between the air on both sides of the tympanic membrane can prevent it from vibrating properly, which impairs the hearing.

The eardrum is connected to a reservoir of air in the middle ear by the Eustachian tube, the other end of which is connected to the oesophagus (gullet) and opens during the action of swallowing in order to allow the air pressure in the ear to equalise with the outside air pressure. However, when there is a rapid change in air pressure, the Eustachian tube remains closed and traps the air, preventing the air pressure in the middle ear from being equalised. The air in the middle ear is absorbed and a vacuum forms, resulting in the feeling that the ears are blocked. This in turn can cause the eardrum to stretch painfully inwards. In many cases, if the tube remains blocked, fluid seeps into the ear in an attempt to unblock the vacuum, giving rise to a condition known as fluid in the ear. The common cold can also block the Eustachian tube because it causes the membranes in the ear to swell, which can block the opening to the tube.

When ears pop, the sound produced is that of the air trapped within the tube rushing out, opening the tube and escaping through the ear. To prevent the air from being trapped in the first place, or to release it and make the ears pop, the Eustachian tube must be frequently opened, which can be achieved by swallowing, chewing or yawning. Babies can force their Eustachian tubes to open while feeding.

Another method of forcing the ears to pop is using the Valsalva technique, named after the Italian anatomist Antonio Valsalva, who invented it in the seventeenth century. The technique involves closing the mouth, holding the nose and then attempting to exhale, which increases the air pressure in the lungs and the throat and blows air up the Eustachian tube and into the middle ear. This makes the ears pop, equalising the pressure and restoring hearing.

WHAT IS CANCER?

Cancer is a collective name given to a group of diseases characterised by causing cells to divide uncontrollably, leading to a destruction of normal tissue and the growth of abnormal tissue. There are over 200 different types of cancer (a Latin word meaning literally 'creeping tumour') that affect different parts of the body.

The multiplication of cells in the body is a normal process carried out to replace dead cells, and the balance between this process – known as *proliferation* – and cell death is strictly regulated by the body. Cancer alters this process, however, and leads to the rapid proliferation of cells, which can produce an abnormal growth called a *tumour*. While benign tumours do not spread or invade other parts of the body, malignant tumours can spread and invade other organs – a process known as *metastasis* – causing the cells of the target organs also to multiply rapidly and destroying their operation. Once vital organs are compromised, a person's life can be threatened and death can result.

Different types of cancer have different symptoms and different treatments. The symptoms of these various forms range from weight loss and excessive sweating to swelling, bleeding and death.

It's thought that risk of cancer is directly affected by both genetic and environmental factors, with particular factors causing (or increasing susceptibility to) different cancers. Environmental factors known to increase the risk of contracting cancer are known as *carcinogens*, examples of which include many compounds present in cigarette smoke (causing lung cancer) and ultra-violet radiation (causing skin cancer). Genetic factors, meanwhile, include a susceptibility to breast and ovarian cancer in women and prostate and testicular cancer in men.

WHY DO YOU NEVER SEE BABY PIGEONS?

In cities all around the world, thousands of pigeons are seen in large flocks on the streets and in the squares, but all of them are adult. So where are all the baby pigeons? Many other infant animals are commonly seen, but never baby pigeons.

Of course, baby pigeons do exist; it's just that they're hidden in their nests, which pigeons build in high-up places, on ledges and on the tops of buildings. Both the male and female incubate their eggs, which hatch after just eighteen days. Baby pigeons need a lot of care from their parents and are fed by both their mother and their father. The parents don't need to leave the nest but feed their young with a glandular secretion called 'pigeon milk', a high-protein food that promotes rapid growth in the baby birds.

During this nesting time, adult pigeons are very territorial and ward off any strangers from their nests, while the baby pigeons remain in the nest and are cared for by their parents until they can fend for themselves. Once this happens, they leave the nest and roam the streets with the other birds. At this stage, they are a similar size to adult pigeons, although they don't reach sexual maturity until five or six months of age. So the truth is that young pigeons are there, although by the time they leave the nest it's difficult to distinguish them from adult pigeons.

WHY DO PEOPLE GET ACNE?

Acne is a common disease of the skin caused by the

inflammation of the skin's sebaceous glands, which can be found in their largest quantities on the face, back, shoulders and chest. Each hair follicle contains a sebaceous gland, which produces an oil that lubricates the skin. Overactive glands produce excess oil, which makes the pores of the skin sticky, preventing dead skin cells from shedding, and this can trap the oil in the follicle, allowing the bacteria there to multiply. The bacteria then produce chemicals that attract white blood cells, causing the skin to inflame – a characteristic reaction of tissues to disease. The inflammation can be accompanied by pus or swelling, and in extreme cases scars can remain once the lesions, or pimples, subside or are removed.

Acne is predominantly caused by a person's adverse reaction to a surge in the male hormone testosterone, resulting in a stimulation of the sebaceous glands, and is therefore most prevalent during puberty. Other causes of acne include stress, particularly sensitive sebaceous glands, irritated skin, blocked and dirty pores, and certain types of drugs, such as steroids and contraceptives.

Acne affects people of all ages and races, although some people are more susceptible to it than others. Scientists don't know why some people suffer from it while others don't, but they think that genetics may play a factor.

Acne can be reduced by keeping the skin clear, while in men a beard can help to reduce it, as facial hair helps to dissipate the oils on the skin. There is no scientific evidence to suggest that a person's diet has any impact on acne; eating chocolate, sugar and greasy foods has not been found to increase the risk of developing it or worsening the symptoms.

HOW DID THE 'MISSIONARY POSITION' GET ITS NAME?

The missionary position is a position for sexual intercourse in which the man and woman lie facing each other, with the man on top of the woman. It is probably the best-known sexual position and has been adopted by people for centuries.

The name of the position is widely thought to derive from the early European missionaries, who discovered that native people in the New World were employing other unorthodox positions, such as the man penetrating the woman from behind. The missionaries taught the natives that couples facing each other was the only position that was acceptable to God (because it was more intimate, enabling both partners to see and kiss each other) and that any other position was considered unnatural. It is generally thought that these teachings were carried out by St Paul, who believed that the woman should be underneath the man during intercourse, while St Augustine also taught that any other position was a sin against nature.

The term was first recorded in its popular definition in the 1960s.

WHY DON'T IGLOOS MELT ON THE INSIDE?

The igloo is a temporary winter shelter built by Alaskan and Greenland Inuits, commonly while travelling on hunting expeditions. It is constructed of blocks – usually measuring 2ft wide by 4ft high and 2in thick – cut from the hard-packed snow and stacked on top of each other in a certain way so that the top of the igloo is rounded to form a dome.

Inside the igloo, Inuits burn oil lamps, which, coupled with the emissions of body heat, can bring the interior temperature up to around 10–15°C. Given this relatively high temperature, far above freezing, it is sometimes wondered why the insides of igloos do not melt. In fact, the inside of the igloo *does* melt, but not to a large extent. When it does melt slightly, the water quickly re-forms as ice on contact with the snow and ice next to it, while the cold outside air and the thickness of the blocks of snow – which, like ice, is an excellent insulator – ensure that they quickly refreeze. This continual freezing and refreezing hardens the igloo and makes it more stable and less prone to melting.

The oil lamps used inside an igloo are burned in a shallow saucer, which prevents the heat from getting too close to the walls of the igloo and melting them. There is also a ventilation hole in the roof of the igloo, and the hottest air and smoke escape through it, reducing the likelihood of the walls melting.

The entire igloo does eventually melt, but not until the outside temperature rises with the change of seasons.

DOES WEARING TIGHT UNDERPANTS AFFECT A MAN'S SPERM COUNT?

Sperm production can take place only at a temperature that is slightly lower than that of the body's core temperature, which is why the testicles hang in a bag called the scrotum, suspended under and away from the body. For this reason, one method of treating infertility is to apply cold water or ice to the scrotum.

Sperm can be easily damaged and need a thermally consistent environment in which to develop properly. If the temperature of the testicles rises too much – for example, if the man wears tight underpants that hold the testicles close to the body or indulges in frequent hot baths or saunas – the excess heat can affect sperm production, reducing the number of healthy sperm produced.

Studies have shown that the average man's sperm count is lower in summer than in winter because of the higher temperatures involved. Further studies have also shown that wearing tight underpants results in a gradual but considerable reduction in sperm count. However, they also discovered that the number of sperm produced increases to normal once the tight underpants are removed, starting with a noticeable increase within two weeks and returning to normal levels after five months.

Studies have also suggested that the material from which the underpants are made is a factor in levels of sperm production. It was found that those made from synthetic material generated electrostatic electricity through the friction generated between the scrotum and the material, reducing the subjects' sperm counts, which again returned to normal once the offending material was removed. Natural fibres such as cotton, meanwhile, were found to have no adverse impact on sperm count.

It has also been discovered that the overheating of testicles is linked to the development of testicular cancer. Also, while consistently wearing tight underpants can reduce sperm count, it's not generally considered to be an effective form of contraception; millions of sperm are released during each ejaculation, so, even with a reduced sperm count, pregnancy can still be achieved.

WHERE DOES THE EXPRESSION 'PIPE DREAMS' COME FROM?

To say that something is merely a pipe dream means that it is not genuinely attainable and is merely a fantasy or unrealistic hope. The expression refers primarily to the dreams experienced by smokers of opium – a narcotic drug that produces an analgesic and hypnotic effect – who inhale the vapours through a pipe, referring to the vivid and fantastic hallucinations often experienced by people under the influence of opium.

The term is thought to have been used in the United States since the late nineteenth century, when opium smoking was still legal, and is believed by some to have been coined by the playwright Eugene O'Neill. Its first written usage, however, was by Wallace Irwin in his 1901 work *Love Sonnets of a Hoodlum*.

WHY ARE PARROTS THE ONLY BIRDS THAT TALK?

The calls and songs of birds are innate and involve no learning. The ability to learn noises by imitating them is present in only three types of birds: songbirds, such as thrushes and lyrebirds; hummingbirds; and parrots.

Of these three types, parrots are the best mimics. It's not known exactly why parrots can mimic and other birds can't, but most experts agree that it's because of the parrot's intelligence and social structure.

Parrots are known to be particularly intelligent birds possessing self-awareness (for instance, being able to recognise themselves in mirrors), which is a characteristic trait of intelligent animals. This superior brainpower, compared with birds such as pigeons and chickens, helps them to imitate the sounds that they hear.

While parrots in captivity mimic the voices of humans, scientists believe that they developed the skill of imitation as a means of survival. Parrots form strong monogamous relationships, and mimicry between partners promotes social bonding, leading to more effective communication and the higher likelihood of producing offspring. Mimicry in larger groups helps to identify members of the group and increases cohesion. As most other types of birds do not have such an advanced social structure, they did not need to develop mimicry.

Male parrots tend to be better mimics than females, possibly because a male parrot who is able to imitate a wide variety is likely to be a seasoned survivor and therefore a suitable mate. Also, a parrot who is able to mimic different sounds and switch between them regularly is likely to maintain a female's interest, while such vocal deftness is likely to prevent predators or rivals from locating it.

Parrots don't have vocal cords and can't actually talk or understand what words mean. Instead, by learning to control the muscles in their throat to change the rate of air flow, they simply repeat the sounds and voices that they hear. Some species are better 'talkers' than others, with the African grey parrot considered the best.

WHY DO PEOPLE SNEEZE?

Sternutation, or sneezing, is a reflex action that expels air from the nose, generally at a speed of greater than 100kph. Each sneeze sends thousands of bacteria-laden droplets into the air, making it an effective spreader of germs and disease, such as the common cold. Because the eyes and the nose are connected, it's almost impossible for a person's eyes to remain open while sneezing.

A sneeze is caused when the nerve endings of the mucous membrane in the nose are irritated, at which point a message is sent to the sneeze centre in the brain, which sends a signal to the relevant muscles that effect the sneeze, expelling the irritation before any infection can result. Dust and pollen are the most common irritants, but any foreign particle can induce a sneeze. Most particles are harmless, but the body mistakes them for parasites and expels them to protect itself. Often the nose mistakes odours or cold air as potential invaders and this can also cause a person to sneeze. Some say that even an orgasm can bring on a sneeze.

Sneezing can also be caused by a swelling of the mucous membrane, which can happen when a person has a cold, for instance, while it's also sometimes caused by sudden exposure to the sun or a bright light, a reaction known as the *photic sneeze reflex*. Scientists don't know exactly why this happens, but the close association between the nerves that cause the sneeze reflex and the eye's optic nerve is thought to be a factor. About one in four people are photic sneezers and it is an inherited trait.

HOW DID APRIL FOOL'S DAY ORIGINATE?

The first of April is known as April Fool's Day, when it's customary to play tricks and pranks on people, although superstition dictates that the pranking ends at noon and any pranks after that time will bring bad luck to the prankster. Anyone who fails to take a joke in good humour is also said to be cursed with bad luck for the following year.

It's not known exactly why this date is recognised in this way or why jokes are played on people. One theory is that it is related to the arrival of spring, when nature 'fools' the world with its temperamental weather, while another theory is that it is to celebrate the fruitless journey of the rook that was sent from Noah's Ark in an attempt to find land.

The most widely held view of the origins of April Fool's Day is that it began in the late sixteenth century, when the Gregorian calendar replaced the Julian calendar. In the old Julian calendar, the year began on 25 March and festivals marking the start of the new year took place on 1 April, because 25 March fell during Holy Week. When the Gregorian calendar changed the new year to 1 January, however, the day continued to be recognised. It is believed that forgetful people who could be tricked into continuing to celebrate the new year on 1 April after the calendar had been changed were known as 'April Fools'. On this date, people would invite others to non-existent parties and events, pretending that the parties were new year's celebrations.

Nowadays, in England the victim of a prank on 1 April is called an 'April Fool', while in Scotland he or she is known as a 'gowk', which means a fool or cuckoo. French people who fall foul of fooling on 1 April are known as 'poissons d'avril', which translates as 'April fish'.

DOES SITTING CLOSE TO THE TV OR READING IN POOR LIGHT RUIN YOUR EYES?

Parents are often heard warning their children about the dangers of sitting too close to the television or reading in bad light, which have both been held as causes of ruining a person's eyesight.

The accusation with which the television is charged might have arisen because of the excessive X-rays that television sets emitted before the 1960s, but there is no medical evidence to suggest that sitting close to a modern set causes any damage to the eyes. Ophthalmology specialists maintain that the eyes of children can focus easily at very short distances without being strained, the only side-effect being possible temporary fatigue. The same is true for prolonged exposure to computer monitors, which causes the eyes to dry out and become tired because people blink less while looking at them. However, further research is being conducted in this area.

Similarly, reading in dim light or watching television in the dark has no long-term effect on a person's vision. Again, adequate light merely reduces the likelihood that a person's eyes will become fatigued.

Some studies suggest that people who are introduced to modern technology from other cultures do experience a high degree of myopia, or near-sightedness. These studies are not conclusive, however, and many believe that any detrimental effects to eyesight are more likely to be as a result of a change in diet.

WHAT IS THE DIFFERENCE BETWEEN MONKEYS AND APES?

Apes and monkeys are often confused and the terms are sometimes used synonymously, although, in fact, while both are primates, they are completely different classes of animal.

The confusion arises because of the similarities in appearance of the two groups. While they're often called monkeys, chimpanzees and gibbons are actually apes, as are gorillas and orang-utans. Similarly, monkeys are often wrongly classed as apes, some even having the word 'ape' in their name.

There are many species of monkeys and they vary considerably in size and appearance. Some live in trees and some on the ground, and their diets range from insects to fruit and leaves. Most monkeys have tails where apes do not.

Apes, meanwhile, have more teeth than monkeys and eat both meat and vegetation. They also have more mobile shoulder joints and arms for brachiating (ie swinging through trees), which most monkeys are unable to do. However, apes' spines aren't as mobile as those of monkeys, who tend to run along tree branches and have the skeletal shape of cats and dogs. Both animals have forward-facing eyes.

In evolutionary terms, apes are far closer to humans than monkeys are, possessing the same basic body structure and exhibiting similar behavioural patterns. They are also capable of using tools, have complex social cultures, are far more intelligent than monkeys and possess impressive language and learning capabilities. Genetically speaking, chimpanzees are the closest living relatives to humans.

WHAT ARE THE SEVEN WONDERS OF THE ANCIENT WORLD?

After travelling the entire civilised Western world before the birth of Christ, a Byzantine mathematician named Philon circulated a paper describing what he considered to be the Seven Wonders of the World.

- The Great Pyramid of Giza in Egypt was a royal tomb built in around 2600 BC. Made of 2.3 million blocks of stone, it is the only one of the seven original wonders that survives today.

- The Hanging Gardens of Babylon were enormous terrace-style gardens built in 600 BC by a king to please his queen. They were situated in what is now Iraq and were reduced to wilderness in around AD 79.

- The Statue of Zeus at Olympia in Greece was sculptured by Pheidias in about 430 BC to commemorate the king of the Greek gods. It was 40ft high and is thought to have been destroyed by fire and foreign armies in around AD 200.

- The Temple of Artemis at Ephesus, in present-day Turkey, was a religious temple built around 350 BC to house a statue of Diana, the goddess of hunting. Many kings of the area helped with the temple, which was destroyed by the Goths in AD 262.

- The Tomb of King Mausolus at Halicarnassus, also in present-day Turkey, was built in 350 BC as a memorial to the king. It was destroyed by an earthquake in AD 1550.

- The Colossus of Rhodes was a statue built on the Greek island in 292 BC to honour the sun god Apollo. It was 120ft tall and was felled by an earthquake in 224 BC.

- The Lighthouse on the isle of Pharos, near the Egyptian city of Alexandria, was built in 200 BC and rose 400ft above sea level, and the light of its fire could be seen 300 miles at sea. It was partially torn down by Arabs and completely destroyed by an earthquake in AD 1375.

HOW CAN YOU TELL IF SOMEONE IS FLIRTING WITH YOU?

In determining whether someone from the opposite sex is flirting and interested in you, the key is to observe his or her body language. It is said that body language makes up over 70 per cent of what people communicate to each other and provides the most genuine indication of a person's thoughts. Women tend to employ subtler body language than men, but both genders emit signals to look out for.

If the person in question is some distance from you and yet is constantly in your line of vision, it's likely that they're interested in you, particularly if they then move closer to you. Similarly, if the person's body and feet are directed towards you, this too is a sign of interest, as is preening – a man straightening his tie or fixing his hair, for instance, or a woman fondling or flicking her hair – if the person does it in your field of vision. Probably the most direct of indirect signals, however, is a person playing 'eye games' with you, glancing at you and then looking away and glancing back. Smiling from a distance and generally appearing open and receptive to an approach are other positive signs.

Meanwhile, there are various non-verbal signals that can indicate interest during a conversation with someone. Smiling by both sexes indicates interest, as does being attentive and appearing interested in the conversation by maintaining a lot of eye contact. A person gazing into your eyes as you talk is an obvious sign of interest, for instance, as is them tilting their head while listening to you. Gestures registering a lack of interest or defensiveness, however, such as crossed arms or backward glances, should be considered negative.

Studies have shown that, if you copy or mirror another's gestures, you will subconsciously build a rapport with them and that they'll be more inclined to like you, so, if you notice a person mirroring what you're doing, it's likely that they're interested in you. Again, if the person's body and feet are openly directed at you and, especially, if they move closer to you and stand in your personal space, this also probably means that they like you. A subtle touch on the hand or arm is also a very strong gesture of interest that can promote rapport between two people.

WHAT ARE THE JFK ASSASSINATION THEORIES?

John F Kennedy was the youngest US president

ever elected, and when he was assassinated in Dallas, Texas, on 22 November 1963 at the age forty-six, he also became the youngest to die. His supposed killer, Lee Harvey Oswald, was arrested and accused of shooting Kennedy from a window on the top floor of a Texas book depository. Oswald maintained his innocence, however, and was killed two days later by a man named Jack Ruby. At this point the US government set up the Warren Commission to investigate the death of Kennedy, and it eventually determined that Oswald acted alone. Some say, however, that there was more than one gunman, and that the theory that the president was hit by a single bullet was flawed because of the way JFK moved once he was hit and the supposedly implausible path and trajectory of the bullet. This led to the idea that the death was a conspiracy and opened the gates for a flood of theories concerning JFK's death.

One such theory has it that the assassination was arranged by the Sicilian Mafia in retaliation for JFK toughening the laws on organised crime in America. This theory is supported by the fact that Jack Ruby had known ties to the Mafia, and some believe that he was hired to silence Oswald. A connected theory is that, as it was known that the Mafia had worked closely with the CIA to try to kill Cuban dictator

Fidel Castro, it was possible that Castro got word of this and orchestrated the assassination.

The security surrounding the vehicle containing JFK was minimal, which led some to believe that the CIA was involved in the assassination, particularly since JFK hadn't fully backed the Bay of Pigs invasion and had apparently threatened to review the CIA's make-up. The car in which he was shot was also quickly cleaned and repaired and his body was immediately flown to Washington, further suggesting that a cover-up was involved. This theory also suggests the involvement of Vice-President Johnson, who JFK was allegedly considering sacking and who had a lot to gain from his superior's death.

Some of the other theories are that J Edgar Hoover organised the killing; the Israeli government did it because JFK was applying pressure on Israel's nuclear programme; and the Soviet KGB killed him because of his stance against communism. Because his body was rushed away so precipitously, some people even say that the assassination never occurred and that JFK's death was staged.

WHEN AND WHERE DID THE GAME OF CHESS ORIGINATE?

Chess is a tactical game played between two people where pieces are manoeuvred on a board comprising a grid of sixty-four alternating black and white squares according to a strict set of rules. It has been described as being both a science and a sport.

A number of countries lay claim to inventing the game. Some say that it originated in China, where a similar game was played as early as 200 BC. Critics of this theory, however, state that Chinese chess is a significantly different game and is unrelated to modern-day chess.

It was also thought by many that chess originated in Persia. However, a set of Arabic manuscripts since discovered suggest that chess was from India. The most common belief now is that chess developed from the game of *chaturanga*, which was invented by a philosopher in India in around AD 600.

Chess spread from India to Persia and then throughout the Islamic world after Persia was conquered by the Muslims, before being transported to Russia, Spain and the rest of Europe. It's now one of the most popular games in the world.

WHY ARE THE TERMS 'BULL' AND 'BEAR' USED IN CONNECTION WITH THE STOCK MARKET?

In stock-market parlance, a 'bear market' is one whose shares are falling and a 'bull market' is one whose shares are rising. These terms have been in existence since the early eighteenth century in London, although their precise origin is uncertain. One theory is that they are derived from the way in which bears and bulls attack their opponents: a bear swipes its paw down while a bull thrusts its horns up.

Another related view is that the terms derive from the blood sports of bull and bear baiting, which were popular in eighteenth-century England and involved a vicious bulldog attacking one of these animals while it was tied to a pole.

The most common theory, however, is that the term 'bear market' is from the proverb 'don't sell the bearskin before you've killed the bear'. Bearskin 'jobbers' in London were the middleman in the sale transaction who, in anticipation of falling prices, would sometimes sell bearskins in order to buy them back later at a lower price. Meanwhile, the term 'bull market' isn't derived from any causal connection with the animal but was the logical opposite to the bear, it too being an animal and often the opponent of the bear in popular fighting spectacles, as well as the most obvious alliterative opposite of the bear. Bulls are also known for charging, which can be interpreted as applying to a stock market that is charging forward.

WHY DOES ALCOHOL MAKE PEOPLE DRUNK?

Alcohol can cause relaxation and happiness if drunk in moderation, and blurred vision, slurred speech and a lack of co-ordination if drunk excessively. In extreme cases, drinking too much alcohol can result in unconsciousness or even death.

Alcohol is absorbed into the water in the bloodstream and carried throughout the body and to the brain, where it interrupts the communication between nerve cells in the brain by altering the neurotransmitter receptors on receiving cells.

Alcohol initially stimulates certain areas of the brain that deal with thinking and pleasure, making them more sensitive to the neurotransmitter glutamine, while also causing the drinker to be more relaxed by increasing alpha-wave activity across the brain. As more alcohol is consumed, it interferes with neurotransmitters in areas of people's brains that deal with motor learning and planning, reducing their inhibitions as well as making them louder and more animated. It also reduces their motor skills, causing them to stumble and sometimes fall.

With a large intake of alcohol, the receptors dealing with pleasure become unresponsive while a chemical is produced that slows down brain activity and leads to memory impairment. Alcohol also suppresses the way in which the brain breaks down glucose, making the brain cells work less efficiently, which results in blurred vision as the cells are unable to process images properly. Alcohol can also change the shape of the cupula (a part of the ear that's responsible for maintaining a sense of balance) to give the drinker the misleading perception that the room they're in is spinning.

The circumstances in which alcohol is consumed can also affect the level of intoxication. Eating a large meal before drinking, for instance, reduces the effects of alcohol because the food slows the absorption of alcohol into the bloodstream, so that the effects of the alcohol on the body's systems are spread over a longer period. People's emotional state can also affect the degree to which alcohol affects them, while studies have shown that people who drink small amounts in places where other people are drunk also exhibit signs of intoxication. This has been found to be the case even when a person has been drinking soft drinks but misled into thinking that the drinks were alcoholic.

WHAT MAKES ANIMALS WARM- OR COLD-BLOODED?

A warm-blooded (homeothermic) animal maintains its body temperature at an almost constant level, regardless of the temperature of the environment, while a cold-blooded (poikilothermic) animal has a fluctuating temperature that depends on the temperature of its surroundings.

Warm-blooded animals (also known as *endotherms*), such as most mammals and birds, generate their own heat by regulating their metabolic rate. They produce more heat than cold-blooded animals, or *ectotherms*, because they have a high metabolic rate and better ways of regulating it than that of poikilothermic animals. They tend to be better insulated, too, being able to retain their heat thanks to a covering of fur or feathers. When the insulation is not enough, they shiver, an action that increases their metabolism and produces heat. Some animals even migrate to warmer climes when the temperature is too cold.

When the environment is too hot, endotherms employ a number of effective devices to cool themselves, such as sweating or panting. In hot conditions they will also move into the shade or cool off in water.

Warm-blooded animals need to metabolise a lot of food in order to maintain their body temperature. Indeed, only a small amount of the food they consume is converted to body mass, the rest being used for heating. However, by maintaining a constant temperature, all of the bodily functions of homeothermic animals operate at all times.

Cold-blooded animals, meanwhile, such as reptiles and fish, have no internal means of regulating their metabolisms and get their heat from external sources, such as the sun, either by basking or – in the case of fish – moving to warmer areas of water in order to increase their metabolisms. Some ectotherms will also migrate to locations with more desirable temperatures. In hot conditions, the blood of poikilothermic animals is hot and they are more active, but, when the temperature cools, they slow down because their muscles are dependent on chemical reactions that take place at a lower rate in cold conditions. If the temperature is too hot, meanwhile, they will seek shade or open their mouths to cool down.

A cold-blooded animal doesn't need to eat much food and converts most of what it eats into body mass, which means that they are able to survive more trying times when food is scarce.

WHY DO PEPPER SHAKERS HAVE MORE HOLES THAN SALT SHAKERS?

While pepper shakers generally have more holes than salt shakers, this wasn't always the case and, indeed, isn't always the case today.

Traditionally, pepper was more expensive than

salt because it wasn't as common and had to be imported. In order to prevent people from using too much pepper, it was therefore put into shakers with fewer holes.

Now that both salt and pepper are inexpensive, salt shakers contain fewer holes than pepper shakers. This is because the grains of salt are heavier and flow faster than pepper. With the faster-flowing salt stored in shakers with fewer holes, the speed of the two shakers evens out so that salt and pepper pour out of their respective vessels at a similar rate.

Some people believe that, because people use larger amounts of salt than pepper on their food, it should be stored in the shaker with the greater number of holes.

DOES PENIS SIZE VARY DEPENDING ON RACE?

The penis sizes of men are frequently discussed and joked about. A large penis is coveted by many, considered a symbol of masculinity and thought to be an attractive quality to women. The size of a man's penis is influenced by a number of factors, such as cold temperatures, which generally reduce the size of the flaccid penis owing to a lack of blood flow causing it to shrink.

Many studies have been conducted on the length

of men's penises. Some are thought to be inaccurate because self-measurement statistics consistently report increased lengths, while those where independent testers have taken the measurements are considered more reliable. Among these studies has been the question of how race affects the length of a man's penis. For many years, people have thought that black men, in particular, have longer penises than those of Caucasian men. While no definitive conclusion has been reached, some studies have suggested that the average black man does indeed have a longer penis than the average white man.

One study found that the average length of the stretched, flaccid penis was 5.2in for white men, 5.7in for black men and 4.2in for Asian men. Another study, meanwhile, found the average length of the unstretched, flaccid penis was 4in for white men and 4.3in for black men. The black men's penises were also found to be longer when erect, but only by 1in, while their circumferences were found to be on average 0.1in larger.

On the basis of these studies, it's evident that the average black man's penis is longer than the average white man's, which is longer than the average Asian man's. Corroborating the latter part of this conclusion is a further finding that American condoms are 7.1in long, whereas Japanese condoms are 6.3in long. For this reason, at one time some travel guides recommended that travellers should take their own condoms when visiting Asia.

WHAT IS THE DIFFERENCE BETWEEN A DONKEY, AN ASS AND A MULE?

The donkey is a hardy long-eared animal that can live on little sustenance in harsh conditions. It was first domesticated over 5,000 years ago by the Ancient Egyptians, who used it for the transportation of goods. This usage spread throughout the world, and today donkeys are still employed for cheap labour in central America, while its skin and meat are also often used.

There are a variety of breeds of donkey (also known as an ass or a *burro*), all of which are smaller than the average horse. A male donkey is known as a jackass while a female is called a jennet. The donkey is sometimes considered to be the domesticated version of the wild ass.

A mule, meanwhile, is the offspring of a jackass and a female horse (or mare), while a hinny is the offspring of a male horse (or stallion) and a jennet. While donkeys have sixty-two chromosomes and horses sixty-four, such hybrids have sixty-three chromosomes and are usually born sterile.

IS SUICIDE ILLEGAL?

The word 'suicide' is a Latin-derived word meaning 'to kill oneself' and refers to the act of intentionally ending one's life. In order to be considered suicide, the death must be the main reason for the act and not simply a consequence. For this reason, so-called suicide bombers and kamikaze pilots are not technically committing suicide.

Attitudes towards suicide vary from culture to culture and religion to religion. Many philosophers in Ancient Greece and Ancient Rome considered it honourable to kill oneself in certain circumstances, while under Islamic law suicide is a sin.

Western civilisation has traditionally looked unfavourably upon suicide, and for many years it was a crime in many jurisdictions. In England, by the tenth century it was considered a crime, and by the seventeenth century anyone who committed suicide forfeited his or her personal property. It wasn't until 1961 that suicide and attempted suicide were decriminalised in England, while in Ireland suicide was decriminalised as late as 1993. Strangely, when suicide was still considered a crime, it was considered punishable by death.

As of 1963, six states of America still considered attempted suicide a crime, but by the 1990s this number was reduced to two states and today suicide is legal everywhere in America. For this reason, the word 'commit' is often avoided in connection with suicide, as it implies that the act is a crime.

While the act of suicide isn't a crime, it can have negative consequences. Most insurance companies, for instance, won't pay out to the beneficiary of a person holding a life-assurance policy who has committed suicide. In addition, many jurisdictions still consider assisting someone in the act – such as a medical professional performing euthanasia – as a criminal offence. Euthanasia consequently remains a hotly debated topic.

HOW DO MICROWAVE OVENS COOK FOOD?

Microwave ovens heat food by bombarding it with microwaves, which, like X-rays and visible light, are part of the electromagnetic spectrum. In ovens, these microwaves are emitted at about 2,500mHz (megahertz), at which frequency they are absorbed by fat and sugar molecules and water in a process called *dielectric heating*, which produces molecular movement in the food and, consequently, heat.

The microwaves penetrate the food evenly, resulting in heat being generated throughout the food as all the molecules are excited at once. This makes heating with a microwave faster than a conventional oven, which uses a method of heat transfer known as conduction to transfer the heat throughout the food. The main disadvantage of microwave cooking, however, is that the microwaves are unable to penetrate deep into thick pieces of food, due to their narrow wavelength, and this can result in uneven cooking. Another disadvantage is that various chemical reactions that cause the browning of food don't exist with microwave ovens because the air surrounding the food is unaffected by the microwaves, and remains at room temperature.

Microwaves don't heat plastic, glass or ceramic because these materials don't absorb them. However, metal actually reflects microwaves, so if metals are placed in the oven the microwaves will bounce off the metal's surface and can potentially damage the oven.

The cooking chamber in the oven is an enclosure called a Faraday cage, which serves to prevent the microwaves from escaping. The door of a microwave oven is composed of glass with a layer of conductive mesh, the width of which is narrower than the wavelength of the microwaves but much wider than those of visible light. This effectively means that the microwaves cannot pass through the door but light can.

The idea for the oven was conceived by Percy Spencer, who noticed that a chocolate bar in his pocket melted while he was working on another experiment involving microwaves. He patented the idea in 1946 and the first microwave oven was built in 1947. The first food to be cooked in a microwave oven was popcorn.

IS HOMOSEXUALITY A GENETIC TRAIT?

The question as to whether homosexuality is genetically determined or a matter of personal choice is a controversial one. Many fundamentalist religious groups maintain that sexual orientation is a product of a person's environment and is a matter of personal choice, claiming that factors such as upbringing and social pressures dictate sexual preference. They also maintain that therapy used to convert homosexuals is effective and that sexual orientation can thereby be changed.

This theory is supported, to a degree, by the concept of adaptiveness. In evolutionary terms, an adaptive trait is one that increases the chances of a species' survival. Homosexual pairs cannot reproduce and so reduce the chances of survival. It is thought by some that, if sexual orientation were inherent, homosexuals would thus have been selected out of the population as it evolved.

Gay organisations tend to support the view that sexual orientation is governed by nature, while many medical professionals also assert that sexual orientation is innate and cannot be changed. While scientists agree that there is no specific 'gay gene', they think that a number of factors are likely to be involved, some of which are probably genetic. Certain studies have suggested that the homosexual male's brain is similar in structure to that of the heterosexual female.

In support of the theory that homosexuality is determined by a person's genetic make-up, it has been discovered that homosexuality is common among animals, especially primates that are closely related to humans. In addition, conversion therapy has been found to be largely ineffective, with a failure rate of over 99 per cent and sometimes leading to suicide, while those who take issue with proponents of the evolutionary argument counter that there are many genetically transmitted diseases that haven't been eradicated through natural selection, so why should homosexuality be any different?

In the absence of any hard evidence supporting either the biological or environmental viewpoint, it's likely that no common view will ever be shared on the topic.

DID DRACULA REALLY EXIST?

The horror novel *Dracula* was written by Bram Stoker

in 1897. While the eponymous character in the novel is fictional, there has been much discussion about his connection with a real-life man named Vlad III Dracula, whom Stoker is said to have read about while researching his novel in the British Museum and on whom some say that the character of Dracula was based.

Vlad III Dracula was also known as Prince Dracula, or Vlad the Impaler. He lived in Dracula Castle and between 1456 and 1462 ruled Wallachia, which bordered Transylvania and is now Romania. While Vlad wasn't a vampire, during his six-year reign he is estimated to have killed up to 100,000 people, his preferred method of murder being that of impaling his victims with sharp wooden stakes. On one famed occasion, he raided Transylvania and slaughtered thousands of people, after which he sat down in the midst of the bodies and enjoyed a hearty meal. He was eventually arrested and imprisoned by the king of Hungary. Today he is considered a folk hero in Romania, but elsewhere he is thought of as a monster who killed for no reason and without remorse.

It is widely believed that Stoker did indeed get the name Dracula from his readings on Romanian history, although many consider that the connection doesn't extend beyond that because the recounting of

Dracula's history in the novel bears little resemblance to the history or nature of Vlad.

DO WOMEN HAVE WET DREAMS?

Wet dreams are dreams of an erotic nature that occur during sleep and are most common in men. They are sometimes called nocturnal emissions because of the ejaculation of semen that accompanies them.

A less well-known fact is that women also experience wet dreams, although no nocturnal emission is present because women rarely ejaculate fluid when they orgasm, which is why few people realise that they exist. Wet dreams are more common in men because the man's penis receives more physical stimulation than the woman's clitoris does during sleep, generally as a result of the man rubbing against bed linen or the bed itself.

During REM (rapid eye movement) sleep, the phase during which people dream, men generally experience a number of erections and women experience vaginal lubrication. If a dream is particularly erotic, both men and women can reach orgasm. While men will often ejaculate, women become aroused in other ways. It is common for their heart rates to increase and their nipples to become erect, while experiencing an increase in blood flow to the genital region, resulting in a swelling of the clitoris and lubrication in the vagina, which can lead to orgasm.

It is estimated that approximately 40 per cent of all middle-aged women have experienced a wet dream or, more specifically, a nocturnal orgasm, while 80 per cent of men are thought to have had a nocturnal emission. While a man's first orgasm is often during a wet dream, most women have already had an orgasm before they experience one during their sleep.

WHY IS THE NUMBER THIRTEEN REFERRED TO AS A 'BAKER'S DOZEN'?

There are a couple of theories concerning the origins of this expression. One suggests that it dates back to the era of Ancient Egypt, a time when bakers were viewed with suspicion as it was common for them to give customers less bread than they had paid for. The penalty for doing this was to nail the baker's ear to the doorpost of his bakery, a style of punishment that continued through the ages. In England in 1266, for instance, a law was passed to regulate the weight of bread produced by bakers. The penalties for breaking this law were harsh, but bakers had difficulty in making bread of a uniform weight and so, in order to ensure that they didn't fall foul of the law, they would place an extra loaf of bread in any delivery. Bakers also tended to be uneducated and not very adept at counting, and so would often send deliveries comprising thirteen loaves rather than accidentally sending only eleven. Another view is that the baker would add a thirteenth loaf as profit for the middle-man vendor who sold his bread.

The expression 'baker's dozen' is thought to have been in existence since 1599, but the practice of including thirteen loaves in a delivery certainly existed well before that time.

WHY DO MEN OFTEN SHIVER AFTER URINATING?

After a man has finished urinating, it's common for him to experience a shiver over his entire body. While this phenomenon is colloquially known as 'piss shiver', it is technically called *post-micturition convulsion syndrome*, and scientists are not exactly sure why it occurs. One theory is that urination results in heat loss after the warm urine has been expelled from the body, or through exposing the penis to the air, causing the body to shiver.

Meanwhile, another theory suggests that the micturition (ie urination) reflex is relayed through the autonomic nervous system, which is responsible for both contracting the urethra to hold in the urine and relaxing it to allow the urine to flow out. It is thought by some that, in order to govern urine retention, the autonomic nervous system produces certain chemicals and that, when the urine is released, the production of these chemicals reduces, and that it is this sudden change in the levels of these chemicals that causes the shivering. Also, as urine is released there is often a change in blood pressure, which might also explain the shivering.

Post-micturition convulsions are generally more acute when a person has a particularly full bladder. They are also more common in men than women, and some find the experience pleasurable or even mildly erotic.

WHAT CAUSES A HEART ATTACK?

A heart attack – known medically as an 'acute myocardial infarction' – is a condition that occurs suddenly and is usually accompanied by chest pain and sometimes a loss of consciousness. It occurs when a coronary artery is completely obstructed, preventing blood flow to the heart itself, effectively killing part of the heart muscle through oxygen starvation.

The major symptom of a heart attack is severe pain or discomfort in the chest, often described as feeling as though the chest is being severely compressed. Sharp stabbing pains can also be felt, as can pains in the shoulders, back and arms. In very mild cases, the victim is even sometimes unaware that a heart attack has occurred.

The most common cause of heart attacks is *atherosclerosis*, a condition where cholesterol and tissue build up in plaques on the arterial wall in or near the heart. The pressure of blood flow can then rupture these plaques, which then block the artery and prevent the blood from flowing. Factors such as smoking tobacco and obesity can contribute to this build-up of plaques.

Heart attacks are also often caused when the workload of the heart rises suddenly – usually due to extreme physical exertion or stress – and insufficient oxygen is supplied to it in order to deal with the increased activity.

Not every episode of chest pain is a heart attack; sometimes it is caused by a condition called *angina*, which is reversible and does not cause the heart muscle to die. Similarly, not all heart attacks result in heart function ceasing; the heart stops beating only in severe cases of myocardial infarction that result in cardiac arrest.

WHY DO SOME BEER HEADS DISAPPEAR FASTER THAN OTHERS?

It is often noticed in pubs that the heads on some

people's beer disappear faster than on others'. There is, in fact, a reason for this.

The head on a beer is beer foam, formed when bubbles of carbon dioxide rise through the beer and attract protein molecules, which cover the bubbles with a skin. The bubbles accumulate at the surface of the beer to produce the foam head, which prevents further carbon dioxide bubbles from escaping, stopping it from going flat.

Different beers produce different types of foam heads. A thick, creamy head is indicative of a high-quality beer containing a lot of protein, producing small and firm bubbles that are stronger and less prone to breaking than those of other beers, which makes the foam head last longer.

The nature of the glass containing the beer also has a bearing on the head that's produced. Some publicans roughen the base of their beer glasses, causing the beer to be agitated on pouring to produce a steady stream of bubbles, which makes the foam remain longer. The shape of the glass is also relevant, as a glass that's wide at the top has a greater surface area and less surface tension than a narrow-lipped glass, resulting in larger bubbles that burst more easily to produce a head that disappears quickly. A glass that's narrow at the top produces the opposite result.

As the beer is drunk, the head will start to disappear as beer is poured through it. Any fatty substance will also reduce the head by attaching to the bubbles and lowering their surface tension, causing the bubbles to increase in size and burst, making the head disappear. Such fatty substances can be present in glasses that are badly washed or bear lipstick smudges, while the grease from a person's mouth – particularly common in pubs selling snack products like crisps and pork scratchings – can also reduce the head. Most soaps and detergents are also fat-based, so, if the glass has been washed with one of these, a thin film of oily residue will remain that will cause the head of the next beer to be poured into the glass to disappear quickly. For this reason, many pubs use special detergents that have been specifically designed for cleaning beer glasses, being low in suds and free of fat.

WHAT IS HYPNOSIS AND IS IT POSSIBLE?

Any definition of hypnosis is usually vague. It is generally considered to be an artificially induced altered state of consciousness where a person is very relaxed and experiences changes in sensations, thoughts or behaviour. It's mainly used as a way of planting positive thoughts in a person's mind that then remain when the person is fully conscious, resulting in an improvement in the person's behaviour. This is what's known as a *post-hypnotic suggestion*.

Some proponents of hypnosis claim that anyone can be hypnotised but that it's more difficult to hypnotise someone against their will, believing that people with good imaginations and who believe in hypnosis supposedly reach deeper hypnotic states than more unimaginative and cynical people, and are more amenable to suggestion and persuasion when hypnotised. Other hypnotists, meanwhile, assert that a person must want to be hypnotised in the first place, and that about one in ten people won't respond to hypnosis.

There are many myths relating to hypnosis that all serve to deepen scepticism surrounding the subject. Supporters of legitimate hypnosis agree that a hypnotised person is still awake and aware of what is transpiring and can generally later remember what occurred. The hypnotist has no control over the person, as many believe, and cannot hold the person in a state of hypnosis for an indefinite period. The subject is always in control of his or her actions and can choose to ignore any suggestions or demands made, and can consciously leave the hypnotic state at any time.

Hypnosis is a branch of science that has attracted a great deal of controversy as well as scepticism. Some studies suggest that only those people who are willing and easily persuaded are susceptible to hypnosis, while following on from this is the critical suggestion that, rather than accessing the subconscious mind, hypnosis merely puts people in a state where they behave the way they *think* a hypnotised person would behave. For example, it has been noted that people undertaking regression hypnosis, who are 'taken back' to their childhood, create false memories because of social pressure and in an attempt to please their hypnotist, suggesting that hypnosis is a social phenomenon lacking any scientific basis.

WHERE DOES THE WORD 'HOORAY' COME FROM?

The word 'hooray', as used in the celebration chant 'hip hip hooray', is a term whose origins have attracted conflicting views.

The word 'hip' was first recorded in English in 1818, but most agree that its origins are still not clear. 'Hooray', meanwhile, is from 'hurrah', which probably derives from 'huzzah', a sailors' cheer from the seventeenth century. 'Hurrah' is also thought to have been the battle cry of Prussian soldiers during the War of Liberation in 1812, deriving from the Slavic word 'huraj', meaning 'to paradise'.

There is a widely held belief that the term 'hip hip

hooray' is of anti-Semitic origin, deriving from the cry of 'Hierosolyma est perdita' (literally 'Jerusalem is destroyed') uttered by the Romans in AD 135 to celebrate the destruction of Jerusalem, upon which people would respond with 'hoorah'. The cry was later shortened to its acronym, the letters HEP, which eventually became 'hip', making 'hip hip hooray'. A similar theory is that the same phrase was used by Spanish crusaders who invaded Jerusalem, although there is little evidence to suggest that either of these theories is true.

Others believe that the term derives from the words 'hep, two, three, four', used by drill instructors in the armed forces, a phrase that might have been extended to 'hep, hep, hooray' during celebrations.

WHY ARE MEN MORE LIKELY TO CHEAT ON THEIR PARTNERS THAN WOMEN?

It's a fundamental theory of evolutionary biology that the male of any species engaging in sexual reproduction, including humans, seeks to have sex with as many different partners as possible in order to increase his chances of procreation. By imposing monogamy on men, Western society has attempted to use moral codes to contradict this innate urge. This conflict between a man's physical biology and society's standards has resulted in confusion.

The male hormone testosterone is the primary chemical that governs human sexual desire. Men have twenty times more testosterone than women, leading them to desire more strongly the short-term pleasures derived from sex. Coupled with this are the evolutionary impulses instinctually present in men.

A man's reproductive success depends on how many women he has sex with: the more mates he has, the more likely it is that his genes will live on. Women, on the other hand, are limited in their sexual proclivities by the number of children they can have and need only one mate to inseminate them, a biological feature that makes them more discriminating in choosing their sexual partners. While men instinctually seek *quantity* of sexual partners, women seek mates of *quality*. Women desire a relationship and commitment and look for men who are not only likely to produce strong and healthy offspring but who will also protect and provide for them.

The structure of both men's and women's brains is geared towards accommodating these instincts. The male brain, for instance, is highly specialised, and specific parts are used to accomplish specific tasks. Men are thus able to separate information and emotions into different compartments; the areas of the brain dealing with love and sex, for instance, are not connected and so can operate in isolation, which means that, for men, sex can involve very little emotion.

Conversely, the female brain is more diffused, the different parts more intricately connected. Women use different parts of their brains for single tasks, and they would need to be closely linked for this to be possible. Notably, the area of the female brain that deals with emotion and love is closely linked to the area that deals with sex. If a woman has sex with a man, her sexual desire is usually coupled with emotions of attachment and love, and it's this cerebral interconnectedness that explains why women have difficulty understanding and accepting men's infidelity.

DO CAMEL HUMPS CONTAIN WATER?

The camel is a large mammal that lives for up to fifty years, can eat virtually anything and can live in very dry conditions. There are two distinct species of camel: *Camelus dromedarius* (or dromedary) and *Camelus bactrianus*, the former having one large hump on its back and the latter having two. The camel is the only animal with this characteristic.

Each hump on a camel's back can weigh as much as 35kg and contains a fatty, fleshy lump (not water, as many people believe), enabling the camel to survive for up to two weeks without food or water. This prominent feature is the direct result of the camel's inability to store layers of fat under its skin; instead, fat accumulates in the hump on its back. When food and water are scarce, the camel uses the fat for energy and nourishment, and, as the fat is used, the hump becomes increasingly flabby and shrinks. Once the camel eats and drinks again, however, the hump replenishes its fat supplies and returns to its normal size.

The camel's hump also serves as a water source. As the fat from the hump is broken down, hydrogen is released, which combines with oxygen to form water. After a prolonged period without water, the camel will drink up to thirty gallons at a time.

WHAT IS GRAVITY AND EINSTEIN'S THEORY OF RELATIVITY?

Gravity, the force of attraction between two bodies separated in space, can be described in basic terms as the tendency of bodies to move towards each other. The reason why this occurs is still not known.

The theory of universal gravitational attraction was first formulated by Sir Isaac Newton, who postulated that every object in the universe attracts every other object with a force directed along the line of the centres of the two objects, while the force of this attraction varies depending on the masses of the two objects and their distance from each other. However, this theory has now been replaced by Albert Einstein's theories of relativity.

Einstein's special theory of relativity, formulated in 1905, states that the laws of physics are the same when witnessed by two different observers in uniform relative motion – which, in short, means that the speed of light in a vacuum will be the same for all observers. His later general theory of relativity, published in 1915, included a theory of gravitation in which he argued that the presence of matter actually changes space-time, which means that gravity is no longer a force, as Newton believed, but a consequence of the curvature of space-time. In effect, Einstein suggested, the presence of mass and energy curves space-time and this in turn affects the path of objects in freefall, including light.

WHAT EVIDENCE EXISTS ABOUT THE LOCH NESS MONSTER?

The Loch Ness Monster is supposedly a large, amphibious creature, said by some to inhabit Loch Ness, a large inland lake situated in Scotland. She is known affectionately as Nessie, and rumours concerning her existence have been heard for hundreds of years. Locals in the area are the most adamant that Nessie exists, and a large tourism industry has been built up around the mythical monster.

The first reported sighting of Nessie occurred over 1,500 years ago, but her supposed existence first came to public attention in 1933, with reported sightings of a large monster swimming on the surface of the loch. Then, in 1934, a photograph allegedly taken by a London surgeon named Robert Wilson presented the image of a huge animal with a long neck. This supposed 'evidence' fuelled the argument for Nessie's existence, but a relative of Wilson's, Marmaduke Wetherell, confessed on his deathbed that the photograph was a fake, admitting that it was a photograph of clay mounted on top of a toy submarine and that Wilson didn't even take it.

Most experts doubt the existence of the Loch Ness Monster, regarding reported sightings as either hoaxes or the result of people innocently mistaking the appearances of seals, logs, boats or surging waves. Meanwhile, the bubbling and water disruptions that have been observed at the bottom of the loch and attributed to the 'monster' could be the result of volcanic activity.

Experts also claim that the animal would need a breeding colony in order to survive, which would result in many more sightings and physical evidence of remains, arguing that Loch Ness isn't large enough to support a colony of monsters.

In the 1970s, a boat crew took some blurry

underwater photographs that suggested something was living in the loch, but an extensive investigation of Loch Ness in 2003 using sonar beams found no evidence of Nessie, effectively concluding the debate concerning her existence.

ARE GREEN POTATO CRISPS POISONOUS?

A common fear among children who eat crisps is that the green ones are poisonous. While most adults dismiss this fear, there is in fact some truth behind it.

When potatoes are exposed to excessive light of any form, it causes photosynthesis to take place, resulting in part of the potato turning green due to the presence of chlorophyll. This process produces a compound called solanine, which is a glycoalkaloid. Normally concentrated in the leaves and sprouts of plants, such compounds are toxic in large amounts. What's more, the toxin isn't destroyed through boiling. Sometimes, potatoes that have undergone this process find their ways into bags of potato crisps, where they can be identified by their green colouration. When eaten in small quantities, while they might result in a stomach ache, these green crisps generally cause no damage.

Brown potato crisps, on the other hand, are produced by using potatoes stored at low temperatures, causing them to accumulate excessive sugar. Brown crisps are, however, harmless.

DO TAXI DRIVERS HAVE BETTER THAN AVERAGE MEMORIES?

To become a registered taxi driver in London, hopeful applicants must undergo three years of intensive training and are required to learn the labyrinth of streets in a six-mile radius of Charing Cross. The course is very strict, and three-quarters of those who enrol drop out before completion.

To learn the layout of the hundreds of streets (known colloquially as 'the knowledge'), taxi drivers are thought to possess memories that are far greater than that of the average person. During studies conducted to determine the accuracy of this belief, imaging scans of the grey-matter density of taxi drivers' brains were compared with images of the brains of other people. These scans found that taxi drivers had a larger hippocampus – the area of the brain associated with memory and navigational abilities – than non-taxi drivers. The taxi drivers' hippocampuses had also changed in structure and had enlarged to deal with the navigational requirements and to store a detailed map of the streets.

Studies also found that the average taxi driver's hippocampus increased in size as the driver spent more time on the road. The longer someone had been a driver, the larger his or her hippocampus.

This evidence of changes and growth in the brain is now being used in an attempt to develop rehabilitation programmes for people with brain damage.

WHAT IS THE DIFFERENCE BETWEEN A HERB AND A SPICE?

Herbs and spices add flavour, aroma and aesthetic appeal to food and, while the words 'herb' and 'spice' are often used interchangeably, they are actually different things.

Generally speaking, a herb is a garnish extracted from the leaves of plants, while spices are derived from their fruit, berries, seeds, bark or roots.

Herb-producing plants consist of flowers, stems and leaves (the latter of which bears a fragrant smell), tend to grow in temperate regions and are used to flavour foods or as medicines. Spices, meanwhile, are derived from dried aromatic plants usually from tropical climates and are used to add flavour to or preserve foods, and they too are also used for medicines. Throughout history, spices were highly valued and often traded. They tend to have a strong and distinct flavour, while herbs are usually milder, greener and leafier.

Examples of spices include cinnamon, ginger,

pepper, nutmeg and mace, while examples of herbs include mint, thyme, rosemary, chives, dill and parsley.

CAN STRESS CAUSE ILLNESS OR DEATH?

Extreme emotional stress is a psychological condition that in certain circumstances can manifest itself in physical symptoms, sometimes causing illness or even resulting in death. It's thought to be the cause of death of many old people who die shortly after losing a partner, being so traumatised by the experience that they too become ill and die.

Scientists have long known that stress can cause illness, but they haven't been able to explain why until fairly recently. It is now believed that stress is linked to the way in which cells and molecules communicate. Molecules known as cytokines act as signalling devices, alerting the immune system to dangers, and it's thought that stress can inhibit this cytokine signalling. Studies conducted on rats have shown that the immune cells known as monocytes would not respond to cytokine when the rats were severely stressed.

The body reacts to stress by releasing various hormones and chemicals, and it's thought that these interfere with the cytokine signalling, causing an inhibition of the immune system that can make the body more susceptible to illness and disease.

HOW CAN WATER BE FOUND IN DRY CONDITIONS?

In dry conditions, explorers and adventurers can face the risk of being without water, and it must be found within two or three days before serious dehydration results, followed by death. There are a number of ways to do this.

Water can sometimes be found by digging in dry creek beds or areas where there is vegetation. It can also lie trapped in the crevices of rocks or in the leaves of plants. Catching rainwater with plastic or bark is also a useful way of obtaining water.

Animals also require water on a regular basis, and so following game trails or flying birds will often lead to a water source. Similarly, ants marching up trees are usually heading towards water in the tree, and flies normally live fairly close to water. In desperate times, the eyes of some animals contain water that can be drunk and large fish often have a reservoir of water along their spine.

Alternatively, tying a plastic bag around the leaves on a growing tree branch can trap condensation, as can a solar still. These devices consist of a hole dug in the ground in which is placed a container to trap the water. A plastic sheet is then spread over the hole, dipping in the middle towards the container, which collects the moisture from the ground that condenses on the underside of the plastic.

Seawater and urine can also produce drinkable water if they are distilled, which can be effected by putting a tube into the top of a filled container and then boiling the liquid. Vapour will then pass down the tube and condense as it goes, whereupon it can be collected as water in a second sealed container.

Any stagnant water found should, of course, be thoroughly boiled before drinking.

WHERE DID THE TERM 'RED HERRING' ORIGINATE?

To be given a 'red herring' is to be provided with a false clue or an item of no practical use. The expression has been in existence since 1884 and derives from the centuries-old practice of curing herrings with salt and smoke in order to preserve them. Once cured, the herring turns a crimson colour and possesses a distinctive and pungent smell.

There are a couple of explanations for the origin of the saying that centre around the smell of the fish. The most common is that British fugitives in the nineteenth century would rub a red herring across their trail, which would disguise their scent and confuse any bloodhounds that were trailing them. Then, by the twentieth century, American investment bankers called preliminary prospectuses 'red herrings' as a warning to prospective investors that the documents were incomplete and potentially misleading.

A second explanation is that red herrings were used to train hunting dogs, being dragged through the trees in order to teach the dogs how to follow a trail. It's said that they were also used to confuse hounds in order to prolong foxhunts.

Another possible origin of the saying is the fact that poachers would use red herrings to throw dogs off the scent of game animals, allowing the poachers the opportunity to catch their prey.

WHAT ARE THE GREENHOUSE EFFECT AND GLOBAL WARMING?

Discovered by Jean Baptiste Joseph Fourier in 1824, the greenhouse effect is the warming of an environment by trapping heat from an external source under a layer of gas and is named after a similar warming effect that occurs in gardening greenhouses. An excellent example of the greenhouse effect in action is provided by the planet Venus, where a thick atmosphere of carbon dioxide locks in the heat the planet receives from the sun. However, the phenomenon exists on Earth as well.

When solar energy hits the Earth, some of it is absorbed and some bounces back. The Earth's atmosphere readily absorbs long-wave infra-red radiation and acts as a blanket, preventing most of the heat from escaping, causing the Earth's surface to warm to a considerably higher level than would otherwise be the case. This effect is known as *global warming*.

Water vapour is the predominant greenhouse gas, but carbon dioxide also influences the greenhouse effect. Both of these factors occur naturally, but many claim that the elevated levels of carbon dioxide caused by the burning of fossil fuels is having a dramatic effect on global warming, making the greenhouse effect more extreme. It is thought that this will significantly increase global warming in the long term.

WHY DOES THE SOUND OF RUNNING WATER GIVE PEOPLE THE URGE TO URINATE?

To many people, the sound of running water provides a strong stimulus to urinate. It's thought that this urge is brought about by the power of suggestion, as running water is associated with flowing urine. Because the sound produced by running water is the same as that produced by an act that people perform many thousands of times over the course of their lives, they are conditioned to associate the sound with urinating, just as one person yawning can cause others to also yawn through the power of suggestion.

However, interestingly the stimulus doesn't have to be sound. Photographs of waterfalls can have the same effect, as can thinking or dreaming about running water. Similarly, placing a sleeping person's hand in a dish of water can sometimes cause that person to wet the bed, as it will evoke dreams about water, resulting in uncontrolled urination.

Urologists generally agree that there is nothing abnormal about this urge. Indeed, it's sometimes used to treat patients with urinary ailments.

WHY IS THE *MONA LISA* PAINTING SO FAMOUS?

Italian Renaissance artist Leonardo da Vinci's painting *La gioconda*, commonly known as the *Mona Lisa*, is the most famous piece of art in the history of the world and is said to provoke instant recognition almost universally. Many songs have been written about the painting, and it is famous throughout the world. Begun in 1504 and finished in 1515, it is believed to be flawless in its detail and virtually perfect. Even while still in da Vinci's studio in Florence, it was inspiring imitations.

The *Mona Lisa* revolutionised painting. For a start, it was the first portrait that depicted its subject from only the waist up; previous portraits were always full length. Also, the background in the painting is imaginary, describing a line of distant hills, which again was different to previous works in the medium. The depiction of the female subject is extraordinarily vivid and, on seeing it, many comment that they experienced the sense that they were looking at a living person. The smile on the woman is often discussed, with many people seeing it in different ways.

The identity of the painting's female subject is also a matter of debate, some believing her to be the wife of Francesco del Giocondo (hence the painting's Italian name), a rich Florentine silk merchant, while others believe her to be a self-portrait of Leonardo or a construct of his imagination.

In the 1530s, the painting was acquired by the king of France, whereupon it was moved in the 1650s to the Louvre Museum in Paris. Then, from 1800, it hung in Napoleon Bonaparte's bedroom for four years before eventually returning to the museum. In 1911, it was stolen from the Louvre by an employee, who was caught trying to sell it to an art dealer in Florence in 1913, and then in 1956 it was damaged in an acid attack. In 1963, it was taken on a tour of America, where it was viewed by over a million people, a figure that doubled on its 1974 tour of Tokyo and Moscow.

The momentum of fame, coupled with the painting's colourful history, has made the *Mona Lisa* increasingly famous. Its current value is estimated as being somewhere in the vicinity of £500 million. The painting now hangs behind glass in the Louvre Museum, where it is viewed by thousands of people every year.

WHY WAS STONEHENGE BUILT?

Stonehenge is a monument situated in southern England comprising a collection of large stones arranged in a circular setting. Its name derives from an Old English word meaning 'hanging stones'. It's widely believed that it was built over a period of 2,000 years, beginning in around 3100 BC, and that its construction involved having the enormously heavy stones laboriously transported from far-off places and then erecting them in a specific design.

There are many theories and suggestions concerning why Stonehenge was built. In the ninth century, it was said that the monument was built as a memorial to noblemen killed in battle, while others believed that it was a Roman temple. It was even believed by some to have had supernatural beginnings.

The stones, or megaliths (literally 'giant stones'), of which Stonehenge is composed are aligned northeast to southwest, which has led many to believe that the monument was originally an ancient solar and lunar calendar, as during the summer solstice the sun rises directly in line with one of the stones when viewed from the centre of the monument. Some also believe that Stonehenge could have been used to predict eclipses in a similar way. In the time that the monument was built, worshipping of the sun was not uncommon, and most experts agree that there is some astronomical significance to the way the stones are situated.

However, many archaeologists now believe that the most likely purpose of Stonehenge was as a sacred site that marked the end of a long funeral procession. They claim that the astronomical alignments of the stones were probably made only for symbolic reasons. Indeed, numerous burial sites have been discovered near the stones, lending weight to this theory.

WHAT ARE CROP CIRCLES AND WHAT CAUSES THEM?

Crop circles are large geometrical shapes and other patterns that appear in flattened areas of agricultural crops. The earliest crop circle was recorded during the seventeenth century when a strange image appeared in a field of corn, but they became famous later in England during the 1970s, when many began to appear in fields all over the country. Since that time, thousands of crop circles have appeared all over the world.

The early crop circles tended to be simple circular patterns, which led people to believe that they were a natural phenomenon, but as they became more common the intricacy of the patterns they described increased, leading some people to think that they were made by extraterrestrial life forms or their vehicles (ie flying saucers) landing in the fields. Others believe that the shapes are caused by high-frequency sounds or vibrations, ball lightning or even the beam emitted by a manmade satellite that heats the stems of the wheat.

There is no evidence to suggest that the origins of crop circles are in any way bizarre, and most experts believe that they are created by people in the middle of the night as pranks. Adding to this belief is the fact that some people have come forward and admitted to creating crop circles, even demonstrating how they do it – usually very quickly and with simple tools such as planks of wood and ropes.

WHY DO PEOPLE SAY 'CHEERS' AND CLINK GLASSES BEFORE DRINKING?

It's customary when drinking in company to clink your glass with others and say 'cheers'. This ritual is said to have been in existence for thousands of years.

The word 'cheers' derives from the Greek word 'kara', meaning 'head', and from the Old French word 'chiere', meaning 'face'. The expression 'to be of good cheer' means, therefore, 'to put on a happy face'.

The origins of the clinking ritual are less precise. In one of his novels, Alexandre Dumas wrote that glasses were clinked so that some of each drink spilled into the other, thus proving that each drink was free from poison. This is held by most people as being nothing more than the fictional creation of an imaginative mind, although it might have occurred in various places and times throughout history.

The most common and widely accepted theory is that glasses were clinked together in order to frighten the Devil and any demons out of the drinks. Lending weight to this theory is the fact that Germanic peoples were said to clink drinking mugs together or on the table in order to stun any ghosts that might inhabit their beverages. For the same reason, other natives were also known to ring bells before drinking.

WHY DO PEOPLE CRAVE SALT, AND WHY IS TOO MUCH CONSIDERED BAD FOR YOU?

Salt is the common name for sodium chloride, a chemical compound used to flavour or preserve food and present in large quantities in the water of the Earth's oceans. It's a mineral that the human body cannot produce by itself but is nonetheless essential to its continued and healthy existence, compelling people, therefore, to crave its taste.

Most tissues and fluids in the body contain salt, which contains electrolytes that carry the electrical currents through the human body (the sodium ions that are contained in salt are used to regulate nerve impulses). These electrolytes are also required for the production of enzymes, which are responsible for the production of hormones, the functioning of muscles and the absorption of nutrients. Sodium is necessary, too, for the production of hydrochloric acid, which is used in the stomach to help break down food.

While the body cannot function without salt, excessive salt intake can lead to serious health problems. When sodium levels are too high, which can occur through ingesting too much salt, the body retains additional water in order to compensate, increasing the volume of bodily fluids. This in turn is thought to expose weaknesses in the brain's blood vessels, which can cause them to burst, resulting in a stroke in extreme cases and mild headaches in minor cases. This increased volume of fluid is also linked to high blood pressure, which imposes an additional strain on the heart and can lead to heart failure in extreme cases. Excess sodium also causes calcium to be lost with urine, which can contribute to osteoporosis, and it can be an irritant to the stomach, increasing the potency of carcinogens that cause stomach cancer and ulcers.

HOW CAN A FIRE BE LIT WITHOUT MATCHES?

There are many ways in which a fire can be lit without the use of matches. Here are a few of the more well-known examples:

- Sunlight can be focused through a magnifying glass or camera lens to form a bright spot of intense light and heat, which can generate a fire when directed to dry leaves.

- A stone made of flint (a mineral found in many areas of the world) can generate sparks when hit with metal such as the blade of a knife. A fire can be ignited by then directing these sparks on to dry leaves or paper.

- It's also possible to start a fire by attaching two lengths of wire to the terminals of a regular household battery. By slowly bringing the bare ends of wire together, a spark will jump between them. Again, by directing this spark to paper, a fire can be ignited.

- Mixing together compounds of potassium chlorate or sodium chlorate and sugar, and then grinding them together to produce friction, can also start a fire.

- One method of lighting fires that has been used for centuries by bush people and natives is the rubbing of a piece of hardwood against a piece of softwood to generate friction, which in turn generates heat and, eventually, fire. There are a number of devices that can be employed to create this friction, the most common being the fire bow, the fire drill and the fire plough, all of which operate via the rapid and continual rubbing of the two types of wood against each other.

WHAT CAUSED THE TWO WORLD WARS?

World War I raged from 1914 to 1918 and was known as the 'Great War', or the 'War to End All Wars'. The rigidity of the various world alliances is often cited as the primary cause of the war.

The Austrian government was worried about its national security because of the increase in territory claimed by the Serbs as a result of the Balkan wars of 1912 and 1913, fearing that Russia would back Serbia in the latter's attempt to annex the Slavic areas of Austria. Then, on 28 June 1914, Franz Ferdinand, who was heir to the Austro-Hungarian throne, was assassinated in Sarajevo by a Bosnian Serb student. As a result of this, the Austria–Hungary alliance, with German backing, demanded that the Serbian government do a number of unrealistic things. The

Serbians would not comply with all of the demands, and so Austria–Hungary declared war, at which point the Russian government, who had pledged to uphold Serbian independence, mobilised its forces. Germany consequently demanded that Russia demobilise and, when she would not, declared war on her and then on her ally France. German forces invaded Belgium on 4 August, which prompted Britain, who had guaranteed the independence of Belgium, to declare war on Germany.

World War II, meanwhile, was a global war that began in 1939 and ended in 1945, the cause of which is rooted in the Great Depression of the 1930s. On their defeat during World War I, the German leaders were compelled to sign the Treaty of Versailles, which saw their country lose most of its territories and have its military restricted, while the country was also forced to make war reparations. As a direct result of this, Germany entered a period of severe unemployment, a time of social unrest that saw the rise to prominence of the Nazi Party under Adolf Hitler, who united the country under a nationalist banner and later formed an alliance with Italy's fascist ruler Mussolini. Hitler defied the conditions of the Versailles Treaty and rebuilt the German military before embarking on a programme of expansion for the German Empire, occupying the demilitarised

Rhineland bordering France. At this point, France and Britain used appeasement and diplomacy to maintain peace, but Germany went on to annex Austria and then Czechoslovakia. When Hitler's forces later invaded Poland, the Allies declared war. Japan eventually entered the war on the side of Germany, while America entered in 1941 on the Allies' side.

WHAT IS THE BEST WAY TO IMMOBILISE OR KILL A PERSON USING BARE HANDS?

In a life-or-death situation, it's possible to immobilise or even kill an assailant with bare hands.

The best and fastest way to immobilise an attacker is to strike at the body's vulnerable areas. A sharp blow with the fist, elbow or knee to the stomach, solar plexus or the testicles of a man will knock the wind out of him and usually render him unable to move, while stamping hard on an attacker's toes or hitting into the back of the knee joints or the kneecap will impede their mobility. A single blow to the back or side of the neck or to the throat can knock them out or render them temporarily unable to breathe. Gouging the eyes with the fingers and tearing at the nose and ears are also effective means of immobilising an opponent, while forcing their hand up hard behind their back will hinder their movements, as will locking your arm tightly around their neck in a headlock.

There are also a number of vulnerable areas on the body, a blow to which can result in the death of an opponent. Hitting under the nose with the heel of the hand and driving the hand upwards can propel the bone and cartilage of the nose into the brain, while a sharp blow to a man's Adam's apple can crush his larynx and asphyxiate him. A hard punch to the temple on the side of the head can also kill, as can breaking a person's neck with a blow to the base of the neck. Hitting a person near the kidneys can rupture a large spinal nerve that's close to the surface of the skin in that region and result in death, while clapping hard across both ears can sometimes burst a person's eardrums, causing them to bleed internally and die.

WHAT IS SEA LEVEL AND DOES IT VARY?

Sea level is generally referred to as mean sea level (MSL), or the average height of the sea. It's measured using a suitable reference surface, a process that involves complex calculations, making an accurate MSL reading difficult to determine.

Mean sea level is not measured at a specific place, but as an average level. It is generally considered to be the still water level, after averaging out the motion of the sea caused by wind, waves and tides. In fact, sea level actually varies in different areas, the sea level at the Pacific Ocean end of the Panama Canal being 20cm higher than it is at the Atlantic Ocean end.

The concept of sea level is based on the assumption that, because all the oceans are interconnected, the water will find its own level. The determination of sea level provides a reference point for the calculation of elevation and altitudes and is vital in the piloting of aircraft.

The mean sea level can vary over time because of changes in the level of either the sea (known as a *eustatic change*) or land (known as an *isostatic change*). In a eustatic change, there is a fluctuation in the amount of water present, usually caused by variations in climate such as global warming causing ice and glaciers to melt, releasing the water locked up in them. An isostatic change, meanwhile, can be caused by volcanic island formation or land subsidence.

In the last 20,000 years, since the last ice age, the mean sea level has risen 120m. From 1900 to 1991, it rose by about 2mm each year, but measurements taken since 1992 calculated the MSL as rising between 3mm and 4mm per year. Since 1999, it has increased even further.

WHY ARE LIONS ASSOCIATED WITH ENGLAND?

The lion is the traditional symbol of England, appearing on the national coat of arms, the shirts of the national football team and the caps of the national cricket team.

For centuries, lions have been popular beasts in heraldry, being associated with Christianity in medieval times and representing justice and power. They have been used on many coats of arms, but the English lion symbol is derived from the Normans, whose symbol was the Lion of Anjou (a former province of France) and who formed the British monarchy.

King Henry I, who was known as the 'Lion of Justice', knighted his son-in-law, Geoffrey of Anjou, in 1127, gifting him a blue shield with gold lions painted on it. The same lions are found on the shield of Geoffrey's grandson, indicating that they were passed down through the ages. Henry I is also thought to have had a royal menagerie that included lions.

The three lions were later used on the second royal seal of Richard the Lionheart, King Richard I of England, who in 1190 introduced the coat of arms, which is thought to have been based on the arms of the Duchy of Normandy. At the time, the Normandy arms used three leopards, which are said to have been confused for lions by the English. From that time until the present day, lions have appeared on the English coat of arms and have been a well-recognised symbol of England.

WHICH CAME FIRST, THE CHICKEN OR THE EGG?

Philosophers have always presented this dilemma as the classic unanswerable conundrum – a chicken can't exist without an egg, and vice versa – but it does have a scientific explanation. It just depends on whether the egg in question is a chicken's egg or any type of egg at all.

If the egg is any type of egg, the answer is straightforward. Over millions of years, some reptiles evolved into a birdlike dinosaur called the *archaeopteryx*. From this animal, birdlife then evolved. The first actual bird resembling a chicken was the mutant offspring of two reptile/bird hybrids that were almost chickens, who laid an egg from which emerged the first chicken-type creature. In this case, the egg came first.

If it is assumed that the egg must be a chicken's egg, the question becomes more complex and its answer depends on what is considered a chicken's egg. Firstly, if a hybrid chicken laid an actual chicken's egg, containing the first chicken, then the egg came first. However, if a chicken's egg is an egg that must be laid by a chicken, then a full chicken must have laid the first chicken's egg, which means that the chicken must have come first.

Combining these two ideas, a third view is that a

chicken must be hatched from a chicken's egg, and that a chicken's egg must be laid by a chicken. In this case, a true chicken must have existed first in order to lay the first chicken's egg, out of which hatched a chicken. This hatched chicken would be the first chicken, despite its mother being the first true chicken.

So, while the answer depends on how the egg is defined, an answer can be reached for every scenario.